As A Man Thinketh

ISBN: 0 68178 943 3

This 2003 edition is published by Borders Press
by arrangement with Grange Books Plc.
The Grange, Kingsnorth Industrial Estate,
Hoo, NR Rochester,
Kent ME3 9ND
United Kingdom
www.grangebooks.co.uk

Copyright Axiom Publishing
www.axiompublishers.com.au

Printed in Malaysia

Grange Books PLC

As A Man Thinketh

by James Allen

CONTENTS

As A Man Thinketh

Who was James Allen?

Although his book, *As A Man Thinketh*, has inspired millions around the world and is partly responsible for launching an entire self-improvement industry, very little is known about its author, James Allen. He was born in Leicester, England in 1864 and worked as a personal secretary for an executive of a large English corporation until 1902. At the age of 38 he retired to writing and moved with his wife to a small cottage at Ilfracombe, England. He penned more than 20 works before suddenly passing away at the age of 48. *As A Man Thinketh* has influenced many contemporary writers including Norman Vincent Peale, Earl Nightingale, Denis Waitley and Tony Robbins, among others.

His 'little volume', as he called it, has been translated into five major languages, inspiring millions of readers to recognise that our visions can become reality, simply through the power of thought.

FOREWORD

This little volume (the result of meditation and experience) is not intended as an exhaustive treatise on the much-written-upon subject of the power of thought. It is suggestive rather than explanatory, its object being to stimulate men and women to the discovery and perception of the truth that 'They themselves are makers of themselves' by virtue of the thoughts which they choose and encourage; that mind is the master weaver, both of the inner garment of character and the outer garment of circumstance, and that, as they may have hitherto woven in ignorance and pain they may now weave in enlightenment and happiness.

James Allen
Ilfracombe, England

THOUGHT AND CHARACTER

The aphorism, "As a man thinketh in his heart, so is he," not only embraces the whole of a man's being, but is so comprehensive as to reach out to every condition and circumstance of his life. A man is literally what he thinks, his character being the complete sum of all his thoughts.

As the plant springs from, and could not be without, the seed, so every act of man springs from the hidden seeds of thought, and could not have appeared without them. This applies equally to those acts called "spontaneous" and "unpremeditated" as to those which are deliberately executed.

Act is the blossom of thought, and joy and suffering are its fruit; thus does a man garner in the sweet and bitter fruitage of his own husbandry.

Thought in the mind hath made us.
What we are by thought was wrought and built.
If a man's mind hath evil thoughts,
pain comes on him as comes the wheel the ox behind.
If one endure in purity of thought,
Joy follows him as his own shadow—sure.

Man is a growth by law, and not a creation by artifice, and cause and effect are as absolute and undeviating in the hidden realm of thought as in the world of visible and material things. A noble and God-like character is not a thing of favour or chance, but is the natural result of continued effort in right thinking, the effect of long-cherished association with God-like thoughts. An ignoble and bestial character, by the same process, is the result of the continued harbouring of grovelling thoughts.

Man is made or unmade by himself. In the armoury of thought he forges the weapons by which he destroys himself. He also fashions the tools with which he builds for himself heavenly mansions of joy and strength and peace. By the right choice and true application of thought, man ascends to the divine perfection. By the abuse and wrong application of thought he descends below the level of the beast. Between these two extremes are all the grades of character, and man is their maker and master.

Of all the beautiful truths pertaining to the soul which have been restored and brought to light in this age, none is more gladdening or fruitful of divine promise and confidence than this—that man is the master of thought, the moulder of character, and the maker and shaper of condition, environment, and destiny.

As a being of Power, Intelligence, and Love, and the lord of his own thoughts, man holds the key to every situation, and contains within himself that transforming and regenerative agency by which he may make himself what he wills.

Man is always the master, even in his weakest and most abandoned state. But in his weakness and degradation he is a foolish master who misgoverns his "household." When he begins to reflect upon his condition and search diligently for the law upon which his being is established, he then becomes the wise master, directing his energies with intelligence and fashioning his thoughts to fruitful issues. Such is the *conscious* master, and man can only thus become by discovering *within himself* the laws of thought. This discovery is totally a matter of application, self-analysis and experience.

Only by much searching and mining are gold and diamonds obtained, and man can find every truth connected with his being, if he will dig deep into the mine of his soul. That he is the maker of his character, the moulder of his life, and the builder of his destiny, he may unerringly prove, if he will watch, control, and alter his thoughts, tracing their effects upon himself, upon others and upon his life and circumstances; linking cause and effect by patient practice and investigation, utilising his every experience, even the most trivial, everyday occurrence, as a means of obtaining that knowledge of himself which is understanding, wisdom, power. In this direction, as in no other, is the law absolute that "He that seeketh findeth; and to him that knocketh it shall be opened." For only by patience, practice, and ceaseless importunity can a man enter the Door of the Temple of Knowledge.

EFFECT OF THOUGHT ON CIRCUMSTANCES

A man's mind may be likened to a garden, which may be intelligently cultivated or allowed to run wild; but whether cultivated or neglected, it must, and will bring forth. If no useful seeds are put into it, then an abundance of useless weed seeds will fall therein, and will continue to produce their kind.

Just as a gardener cultivates his plot, keeping it free from weeds, and growing the flowers and fruits which he requires, so may a man tend the garden of his mind, weeding out all the wrong, useless and impure thoughts, and cultivating toward perfection the flowers and fruits of right, useful and pure thoughts. By pursuing this process, a man sooner or later discovers that he is the master gardener of his soul, the director of his life. He also reveals, within himself, the flaws of thought, and understands, with ever-increasing accuracy, how the thought forces and mind elements operate in the shaping of character, circumstances, and destiny.

Thought and character are one, and as character can only manifest and discover itself through environment and circumstance, the outer conditions of a person's life will always be found to be harmoniously related to his inner state. This does not mean that a man's circumstances at any given time are an indication of his *entire* character, but that those circumstances are so intimately connected with some vital thought element within himself that, for the time being, they are indispensable to his development.

Every man is where he is by the law of his being; the thoughts which he has built into his character have brought him there, and in the arrangement of his life there is no element of chance, but all is the result of a law which cannot err. This is just as true of those who feel "out of harmony" with their surroundings as of those who are contented with them.

As a progressive and evolving being, man is where he is that he may learn that he may grow; and as he learns the spiritual lesson which any circumstance contains for him, it passes away and gives place to other circumstances.

Man is buffeted by circumstances so long as he believes himself to be the creature of outside conditions, but when he realises that he is a creative power, and that he may command the hidden soil and seeds of his being out of which circumstances grow; he then becomes the rightful master of himself.

That circumstances *grow* out of thought every man knows who has for any length of time practiced self-control and self-purification, for he will have noticed that the alteration in his circumstances has been in exact ratio with his altered mental condition. So true is this that when a man earnestly applies himself to remedy the defects in his character, and makes swift and marked progress, he passes rapidly through a succession of vicissitudes.

The soul attracts that which it secretly harbours; that which it loves, and also that which it fears; it reaches the height of its cherished aspirations; it falls to the level of its unchastened desires and circumstances are the means by which the soul receives it own.

Every thought seed sown or allowed to fall into the mind, and to take root there, produces its own, blossoming sooner or later into act, and bearing its own fruitage of opportunity and circumstance. Good thoughts bear good fruit, bad thoughts bad fruit.

The outer world of circumstances shapes itself to the inner world of thought, and both pleasant and unpleasant external conditions are factors which make for the ultimate good of the individual. As the reaper of his own harvest, man learns both of suffering and bliss.

Following the inmost desires, aspirations, thoughts, by which he allows himself to be dominated (pursuing the will-o'-the wisps of impure imaginings or steadfastly walking the highway of strong and high endeavour), a man at last arrives at their fruition and fulfilment in the outer conditions of his life. The laws of growth and adjustment everywhere obtain.

A man does not come to the alms-house or the jail by the tyranny of fate or circumstance, but by the pathway of grovelling thoughts and base desires. Nor does a pure-minded man fall suddenly into crime by stress of any mere external force; the criminal thought had long been secretly fostered in the heart, and the hour of opportunity revealed its gathered power.

Circumstance does not make the man; it reveals him to himself. No such conditions can exist as descending into vice and its attendant sufferings apart from vicious inclinations, or ascending into virtue and its pure happiness without the continued cultivation of virtuous aspirations; and man, therefore, as the lord and master of thought, is the maker of himself and the shaper of and author of environment. Even at birth the soul comes of its own and through every step of its earthly pilgrimage it attracts those combinations of conditions which reveal itself, which are the reflections of its own purity and impurity, its strength and weakness.

Men do not attract that which they *want*, but that which they *are*. Their whims, fancies, and ambitions are thwarted at every step, but their inmost thoughts and desires are fed with their own food, be it foul or clean. Man is manacled only by himself; thought and action are the jailors of Fate—they imprison, being base; they are also the angels of Freedom—they liberate, being noble. Not what he wished and prays for does a man get, but what he justly earns. His wishes and prayers are only gratified and answered when they harmonise with his thoughts and actions.

In the light of this truth what, then, is the meaning of "fighting against circumstances"? It means that a man is continually revolting against an effect without, while all the time he is nourishing and preserving its cause in his heart. That cause may take the form of a conscious vice or an unconscious weakness; but whatever it is, it stubbornly retards the efforts of its possessor, and thus calls aloud for remedy.

Men are anxious to improve their circumstances, but are unwilling to improve themselves; they therefore remain bound. The man who does not shrink from self-crucifixion can never fail to accomplish the object upon which his heart is set. This is as true of earthly as of heavenly things. Even the man whose sole object is to acquire wealth must be prepared to make great personal sacrifices before he can accomplish his object; and how much more so he who would realise a strong and well-poised life?

Here is a man who is wretchedly poor. He is extremely anxious that his surroundings and home comforts should be improved, yet all the time he shirks his work, and considers he is justified in trying to deceive his employer on the ground of insufficiency of his wages. Such as man does not understand the simplest rudiments of those principles which are the basis of true prosperity, and is not only totally unfitted to rise out of his wretchedness, but is actually attracting to himself a still deeper wretchedness by dwelling in and acting out, indolent, deceptive, and unmanly thoughts.

Here is a rich man who is the victim of a painful and persistent disease as the result of gluttony. He is willing to give large sums of money to get rid of it, but he will not sacrifice his gluttonous desires. He wants to gratify his taste for rich and unnatural foods and have his health as well. Such a man is totally unfit to have health, because he has not yet learned the first principles of healthy life.

Here is an employer of labour who adopts crooked measures to avoid paying the regulation wage, and, in the hope of making larger profits, reduces the wages of his workpeople. Such a man is altogether unfitted for prosperity, and when he finds himself bankrupt, both as regards reputation and riches, he blames circumstances, not knowing that he is the sole author of his condition.

I have introduced these three cases merely as illustrative of the truth that man is the causer (though nearly always unconsciously) of his circumstances, and that, while aiming at a good end, he is continually frustrating its accomplishment by encouraging thoughts and desires which cannot possibly harmonise with that end. Such cases could be multiplied and varied almost indefinitely, but this is not necessary, as the reader can, if he so resolves, trace the action of the laws of thought in his own mind and life, and until this is done, mere external facts cannot serve as a ground of reasoning.

Circumstances, however, are so complicated, thought is so deeply rooted, and the conditions of happiness vary so vastly with individuals, that a man's *entire* soul condition (although it may be known to himself) cannot be judged by another from the external aspect of his life alone.

A man may be honest in certain directions, yet suffer privations; a man may be dishonest in certain directions, yet acquire wealth; but the conclusion usually formed that the one man fails because of his particular honesty, and that the other prospers because of his particular dishonesty, is the result of a superficial judgment, which assumes that the dishonest man is almost totally corrupt, and the honest man almost entirely virtuous. In the light of a deeper knowledge and wider experience, such judgment is found to be erroneous. The dishonest man may have some admirable virtues which the other does not possess; and the honest man obnoxious vices which are absent in the other. The honest man reaps the good results of his honest thoughts and acts; he also brings upon himself the sufferings which vices produce. The dishonest man likewise garners his own suffering and happiness.

It is pleasing to human vanity to believe that one suffers because of one's virtue; but not until a man has extirpated every sickly, bitter, and impure thought from his soul, can he be in a position to know and declare that his sufferings are the result of his good, and not of his bad qualities; and on the way to, yet long before he has reached that supreme perfection, he will have found, working in his mind and life, the Great Law which is absolutely just, and which cannot, therefore, give good for evil, evil for good. Possessed of such knowledge, he will then know, looking back upon his past ignorance and blindness, that his life is, and always was, justly ordered, and that all his past experiences, good and bad, were the equitable outworking of his evolving, yet unevolved self.

Good thoughts and actions can never produce bad results; bad thoughts and actions can never produce good results. This is but saying that nothing can come from corn but corn, nothing from nettles but nettles. Men understand this law in the natural world, and work with it; but few understand it in the mental and moral world (though its operation there is just as simple and undeviating), and they, therefore, do not cooperate with it.

Suffering is *always* the effect of wrong thought in some direction. It is an indication that the individual is out of harmony with himself, with the law of his being. The sole and supreme use of suffering is to purify, to burn out all that is useless and impure. Suffering ceases for him who is pure. There could be no object in burning gold after the dross had been removed, and a perfectly pure and enlightened being could not suffer.

The circumstances which a man encounters with suffering are the result of his own mental inharmony. The circumstances which a man encounters with blessedness are the result of his own mental harmony. Blessedness, not material possessions, is the measure of right thought; wretchedness, not lack of material possessions, is the measure of wrong thought. A man may be cursed and rich; he may be blessed and poor. Blessedness and riches are only joined together when the riches are rightly and wisely used. And the poor man only descends into wretchedness when he regards his lot as a burden unjustly imposed.

Indigence and indulgence are the two extremes of wretchedness. They are both equally unnatural and the result of mental disorder. A man is not rightly conditioned until he is a happy, healthy, and prosperous being; and happiness, health, and prosperity are the result of a harmonious adjustment of the inner with the outer of the man with his surroundings.

A man only begins to be a man when he ceases to whine and revile, and commences to search for the hidden justice which regulates his life. And he adapts his mind to that regulating factor, he ceases to accuse others as the cause of his condition, and builds himself up in strong and noble thoughts; ceases to kick against circumstances, but beings to use them as aids to his more rapid progress, and as a means of discovering the hidden powers and possibilities within himself.

Law, not confusion, is the dominating principle in the universe. Justice, not injustice, is the soul and substance of life. Righteousness, not corruption, is the molding and moving force in the spiritual government of the world. This being so, man has but to right himself to find that the universe is right. And during the process of putting himself right, he will find that as he alters his thoughts towards things and other people, things and other people will alter towards him.

The proof of this truth is in every person, and it therefore admits of easy investigation by systematic introspection and self-analysis. Let a man radically alter his thoughts, and he will be astonished at the rapid transformation it will effect in the material conditions of his life.

Men imagine that thought can be kept secret, but it cannot. It rapidly crystallises into habit, and habit solidifies into circumstance. Bestial thoughts crystallise into habits of drunkenness and sensuality, which solidify into circumstances of destitution and disease. Impure thoughts of every kind crystallise into enervating and confusing habits, which solidify into distracting and adverse circumstances. Thoughts of fear, doubt, and indecision crystallise into weak, unmanly, and irresolute habits, which solidify into circumstances of failure, indigence, and slavish dependence.

Lazy thoughts crystallise into weak, habits of uncleanliness and dishonesty, which solidify into circumstances of foulness and beggary. Hateful and condemnatory thoughts crystallise into habits of accusation and violence, which solidify into circumstances of injury and persecution. Selfish thoughts of all kinds crystallise into habits of self-seeking, which solidify into distressful circumstances.

On the other hand, beautiful thoughts of all kinds crystallise into habits of grace and kindliness, which solidify into genial and sunny circumstances. Pure thoughts crystallise into habits of temperance and self-control, which solidify into circumstances of repose and peace. Thoughts of courage, self-reliance, and decision crystallise into manly habits, which solidify into circumstances of success, plenty, and freedom.

Energetic thoughts crystallise into habits of cleanliness and industry, which solidify into circumstances of pleasantness. Gentle and forgiving thoughts crystallise into habits of gentleness, which solidify into protective and preservative circumstances. Loving and unselfish thoughts solidify into circumstances of sure and abiding prosperity and true riches.

A particular train of thought persisted in, be it good or bad, cannot fail to produce its results on the character and circumstances. A man cannot *directly* choose his circumstances, but he can choose his thoughts, and so indirectly, yet surely, shape his circumstances.

Nature helps every man to gratification of the thoughts which he most encourages, and opportunities are presented which will most speedily bring to the surface both the good and the evil thoughts.

Let a man cease from his sinful thoughts, and all the world will soften towards him, and be ready to help him. Let him put away his weakly and sickly thoughts, and the opportunities will spring up on every hand to aid his strong resolves. Let him encourage good thoughts, and no hard fate shall bind him down to wretchedness and shame. The world is your kaleidoscope, and the varying combinations of colours which at every succeeding moment it presents to you are the exquisitely adjusted pictures of your ever-moving thoughts.

"You will be what you will to be;
Let failure find its false content
In that poor word, 'environment,'
But spirit scorns it, and is free.

It masters time, it conquers space;
It cows that boastful trickster, Chance,
And bids the tyrant Circumstance
Uncrown, and fill a servant's place.

The human Will, that force unseen,
The offspring of a deathless Soul,
Can hew a way to any goal,
Though walls of granite intervene.

Be not impatient in delay,
But wait as one who understands;
When spirit rises and commands,
The gods are ready to obey."

EFFECTS OF THOUGHTS ON HEALTH AND BODY

The body is the servant of the mind. It obeys the operations of the mind, whether they be deliberately chosen or automatically expressed. At the bidding of unlawful thoughts the body sinks rapidly into disease and decay; at the command of glad and beautiful thoughts it becomes clothed with youthfulness and beauty .

Disease and health, like circumstances, are rooted in thought. Sickly thoughts will express themselves through a sickly body. Thoughts of fear have been known to kill a man as speedily as a bullet and they are continually killing thousands of people just as surely though less rapidly. The people who live in fear of disease are the people who get it. Anxiety quickly demoralises the whole body, and lays it open to the entrance of disease; while impure thoughts, even if not physically indulged, will soon shatter the nervous system.

Strong pure, and happy thoughts build up the body in vigour and grace. The body is a delicate and plastic instrument, which responds readily to the thoughts by which it is impressed, and habits of thought will produce their own effects, good or bad, upon it.

Men will continue to have impure and poisoned blood, so long as they propagate unclean thoughts. Out of a clean heart comes a clean life and a clean body. Out of a defiled mind proceeds a defiled life and a corrupt body. Thought is the fount of action, life and manifestation; make the fountain pure, and all will be pure.

Change of diet will not help a man who will not change his thoughts. When a man makes his thoughts pure, he no longer desires impure food.

Clean thoughts make clean habits. The so-called saint who does not wash his body is not a saint. He who has strengthened and purified his thoughts does not need to consider the malevolent microbe.

If you would perfect your body, guard your mind. If you would renew your body, beautify your mind. Thoughts of malice, envy, and disappointment, despondency, rob the body of its health and grace. A sour face does not come by chance; it is made by sour thoughts. Wrinkles that mar are drawn by folly, passion, pride.

I know a woman of ninety-six who has the bright, innocent face of a girl. I know a man well under middle age whose face is drawn into in-harmonious contours. The one is the result of a sweet and sunny disposition; the other is the outcome of passion and discontent.

As you cannot have a sweet and wholesome abode unless you admit the air and sunshine freely into your rooms, so a strong body and a bright, happy, or serene countenance can only result from the free admittance into the mind of thoughts of joy and goodwill and serenity.

On the faces of the aged there are wrinkles made by sympathy, others by strong and pure thought, and others are carved by passion; who cannot distinguish them? With those who have lived righteously, age is calm, peaceful, and softly mellowed, like the setting sun. I have recently seen a philosopher on his death-bed. He was not old except in years. He died as sweetly and peacefully as he had lived.

There is no physician like cheerful thought for dissipating the ills of the body; there is no comforter to compare with goodwill for dispersing the shadows of grief and sorrow. To live continually in thoughts of ill will, cynicism, suspicion, and envy, is to be confined in a self-made prison hole. But to think well of all, to be cheerful with all, to patiently learn to find the good in all—such unselfish thoughts are the very portals of heaven; and to dwell day by day in thoughts of peace toward every creature will bring abounding peace to their possessor.

THOUGHT AND PURPOSE

Until thought is linked with purpose there is no intelligent accomplishment. With the majority the bark of thought is allowed to "drift" upon the ocean of life. Aimlessness is a vice, and such drifting must not continue for him who would steer clear of catastrophe and destruction.

They who have no central purpose in their life fall an easy prey to petty worries, fears, troubles, and self-pityings, all of which are indications of weakness, which lead, just as surely as deliberately planned sins (though by a different route), to failure, unhappiness, and loss, for weakness cannot persist in a power-evolving universe.

A man should conceive of a legitimate purpose in his heart, and set out to accomplish it. He should make this purpose the centralising point of his thoughts. It may take the form of a spiritual ideal, or it may be a worldly object, according to his nature at the time being. Whichever it is, he should steadily focus his thought forces upon the object he had set before him. He should make this purpose his supreme duty and should devote himself to its attainment, not allowing his thoughts to wander away into ephemeral fancies, longings, and imaginings\ This is the royal road to self-control and true concentration of thought. Even if he fails again and again to accomplish his purpose—as he must until weakness is overcome—the strength of character gained will be the measure of his *true* success, and this will form a new starting point for future power and triumph.

Those who are not prepared for the apprehension of a great purpose, should fix the thoughts upon the faultless performance of their duty, no matter how insignificant their task may appear. Only in this way can the thoughts be gathered and focused, and resolution and energy be developed. Once this is done, there is nothing which may not be accomplished.

The weakest soul knowing its own weakness, and believing this truth—*that strength can only be developed by effort and practice*—will, thus believing, at once begin to exert itself. And, adding effort to effort, patience to patience, and strength to strength, will never cease to develop and will at last grow divinely strong.

As the physically weak man can make himself strong by careful and patient training, so the man of weak thoughts can make them strong by exercising himself in right thinking.

To put away aimlessness and weakness and to begin to think with purpose, is to enter the ranks of those strong ones who only recognise failure as one of the pathways to attainment. Who make all conditions serve them, and who think strongly, attempt fearlessly, and accomplish masterfully.

Having conceived of his purpose, a man should mentally mark out a straight pathway to its achievement, looking neither to the right nor left. Doubts and fears should be rigorously excluded. They are disintegrating elements which break up the straight line of effort, rendering it crooked, ineffectual, useless. Thoughts of doubt and fear can never accomplish anything. They always lead to failure. Purpose, energy, power to do, and all strong thoughts cease when doubt and fear creep in.

The will to do springs from the knowledge that we can do. Doubt and fear are the great enemies of knowledge, and he who encourages them, who does not slay them, thwarts himself at every step.

He who has conquered doubt and fear has conquered failure. His every thought is allied with power, and all difficulties are bravely met and overcome. His purposes are seasonably planted, and they bloom and bring forth fruit that does not fall prematurely to the ground.

Thought allied fearlessly to purpose becomes creative force. He who *knows* this is ready to become something higher and stronger than a bundle of wavering thoughts and fluctuating sensations. He who *does* this has become the conscious and intelligent wielder of his mental powers.

∂

THE THOUGHT-FACTOR IN ACHIEVEMENT

All that a man achieves and all that he fails to achieve is the direct result of his own thoughts. In a justly ordered universe, where loss of equipoise would mean total destruction, individual responsibility must be absolute. A man's weakness and strength, purity and impurity, are his own and not another man's. They are brought about by himself and not by another; and they can only be altered by himself, never by another. His condition is also his own, and not another man's. His sufferings and his happiness are evolved from within. As he thinks, so is he; as he continues to think, so he remains.

A strong man cannot help a weaker unless that weaker is *willing* to be helped. And even then the weak man must become strong of himself. He must, by his own efforts, develop the strength which he admires in another. None but himself can alter his condition.

It has been usual for men to think and to say, "Many men are slaves because one is an oppressor; let us hate the oppressor!" But there is amongst an increasing few a tendency to reverse this judgement and to say, "One man is an oppressor because many are slaves; let us despise the slaves." The truth is that oppressor and slaves are cooperators in ignorance, and, while seeming to afflict each other, are in reality, afflicting themselves. A perfect knowledge perceives the action of law in the weakness of the oppressed and the misapplied power of the oppressor. A perfect love, seeing the suffering which both states entail, condemns neither; a perfect compassion embraces both oppressor and oppressed.

He who has conquered weakness and has pushed away all selfish thoughts belongs neither to oppressor nor oppressed. He is free.

A man can only rise, conquer, and achieve by lifting up his thoughts. He can only remain weak, and abject, and miserable by refusing to lift up his thoughts.

Before a man can achieve anything, even in worldly things, he must lift his thoughts above slavish animal indulgence. He may not, in order to succeed, give up all animality and selfishness, necessarily, but a portion of it must, at least, be sacrificed. A man whose first thought is bestial indulgence could neither think clearly nor plan methodically. He could not find and develop his latent resources and would fail in any undertaking. Not having begun to manfully control his thoughts, he is not in a position to control affairs and to adopt serious responsibilities. He is not fit to act independently and stand alone. But he is limited only by the thoughts that he chooses.

There can be no progress nor achievement without sacrifice, and a man's worldly success will be by the measure that he sacrifices his confused animal thoughts, and fixes his mind on the development of his plans, and the strengthening of his resolution and self-reliance. The higher he lifts his thoughts, the greater will be his success, the more blessed and enduring will be his achievements.

The universe does not favour the greedy, the dishonest, the vicious, although on the mere surface it sometimes may appear to do so. It helps the honest, the magnanimous, the virtuous. All the great teachers of the ages have declared this in varying forms, and to prove it and to know it a man has but to persist in making himself increasingly virtuous by lifting his thoughts.

Intellectual achievements are the result of thought consecrated to the search for knowledge or for the beautiful and true in nature. Such achievements may sometimes be connected with vanity and ambition, but they are not the outcome of those characteristics. They are the natural outgrowth of long and arduous effort, and of pure and unselfish thoughts.

Spiritual achievements are the consummation of holy aspirations. He who lives constantly in the conception of noble and lofty thoughts, who dwells upon all that is pure and selfless, will, as surely as the sun reaches its zenith and the moon its full, become wise and noble in character and rise into a position of influence and blessedness.

Achievement of any kind is the crown of effort, the diadem of thought. By the aid of self-control, resolution, purity, righteousness, and well-directed thought a man ascends. By the aid of animality, indolence, impurity, corruption, and confusion of thought a man descends.

A man may rise to high success in the world, even to lofty attitudes in the spiritual realm, and again descend into weakness and wretchedness by allowing arrogant, selfish, and corrupt thoughts to take possession of him.

Victories attained by right thought can be maintained only by watchfulness. Many give way when success is assured, and rapidly fall back into failure.

All achievements, whether in the business, intellectual, or spiritual world, are the result of definitely directed thought, are governed by the same law, and are of the same method. The only difference is in the object of attainment.

He who would accomplish little need sacrifice little; he who would achieve much must sacrifice much. He who would attain highly must sacrifice greatly.

VISIONS AND IDEALS

The dreamers are the saviours of the world. As the visible world is sustained by the invisible, so men, through all their trials and sins and sordid vocations, are nourished by the beautiful visions of their solitary dreamers. Humanity cannot forget its dreamers; it cannot let their ideals fade and die; it lives in them; it knows them as the *realities* which it shall one day see and know.

Composer, sculptor, painter, poet, prophet, sage, these are the makers of the afterworld, the architects of heaven. The world is beautiful because they have lived. Without them, laboring humanity would perish.

He who cherishes a beautiful vision, a lofty ideal in his heart, will one day realise it. Columbus cherished a vision of another world and he discovered it. Copernicus fostered the vision of a multiplicity of worlds and a wider universe, and he revealed it. Buddha beheld the vision of a spiritual world of stainless beauty and perfect peace, and he entered into it.

Cherish your visions; cherish your ideals. Cherish the music that stirs in your heart, the beauty that forms in your mind, the loveliness that drapes your purest thoughts. For out of them will grow all delightful conditions, all heavenly environment; of these, if you but remain true to them, your world will at last be built.

To desire is to obtain; to aspire is to achieve. Shall man's basest desires receive the fullest measure of gratification, and his purest aspirations starve for lack of sustenance? Such is not the Law. Such a condition can never obtain— "Ask and receive."

Dream lofty dreams, and as you dream, so shall you become. Your vision is the promise of what you shall one day be; your ideal is the prophecy of what you shall at last unveil.

The greatest achievement was at first and for a time a dream. The oak sleeps in the acorn; the bird waits in the egg. And in the highest vision of a soul a waking angel stirs. Dreams are the seedlings of realities.

Your circumstances may be uncongenial, but they shall not remain so if you only perceive an ideal and strive to reach it. You can't travel within and stand still without. Here is a youth hard pressed by poverty and labour. Confined long hours in an unhealthy workshop; unschooled and lacking all the arts of refinement. But he dreams of better things. He thinks of intelligence, or refinement, of grace and beauty. He conceives of, mentally builds up, an ideal condition of life. The wider liberty and a larger scope takes possession of him; unrest urges him to action, and he uses all his spare times and means to the development of his latent powers and resources.

Very soon so altered has his mind become that the workshop can no longer hold him. It has become so out of harmony with his mind-set that it falls out of his life as a garment is cast aside. And with the growth of opportunities that fit the scope of his expanding powers, he passes out of it altogether.

Years later we see this youth as a grown man. We find him a master of certain forces of the mind that he wields with world-wide influence and almost unequaled power. In his hands he holds the cords of gigantic responsibilities; he speaks and lives are changed; men and women hang upon his words and remold their characters. Sun-like, he becomes the fixed and luminous centre around which innumerable destinies revolve. He has become the vision of his youth. He has become one with his ideal.

And you too, youthful reader, will realise the vision (not just the idle wish) of your heart, be it base or beautiful, or a mixture of both, for you will always gravitate toward that which you, secretly, most love. Into your hands will be placed the exact results of your own thoughts. You will receive that which you earn; no more, no less. Whatever your present environment may be, you will fall, remain, or rise with your thoughts—your vision, your ideal. You will become as small as your controlling desire; as great as your dominant aspiration.

In the beautiful words of Stanton Kirkham Davis, "You may be keeping accounts, and presently you shall walk out of the door that for so long has seemed to you the barrier of your ideals, and shall find yourself before an audience—the pen still behind your ear, the ink stains on your fingers—and then and there shall pour out the torrent of your inspiration. You may be driving sheep, and you shall wander to the city—bucolic and open mouthed; shall wander under the intrepid guidance of the spirit into the studio of the master, and after a time he shall say, 'I have nothing more to teach you.' And now you have become the master, you did so recently dream of great things while driving sheep. You shall lay down the saw and the plane to take upon yourself the regeneration for the world."

The thoughtless, the ignorant, and the indolent, seeing only the apparent effects of things and not the things themselves, talk of luck, of fortune, and chance. Seeing a man grow rich, they say, "How lucky he is!" Observing another become skilled intellectually, they exclaim, "How highly favoured he is!" And noting the saintly character and wide influence of another, they remark, "How chance helps him at every turn!"

They do not see the trials and failures and struggles which these men have voluntarily encountered in order to gain their experience; have no knowledge of the sacrifices they have made, of the undaunted efforts they have put forth, of the faith they have exercised so that they might overcome the apparently insurmountable and realise the vision of their heart. They do not know the darkness and the heartaches; they only see the light and joy, and call it "luck"; do not see the long, arduous journey, but only behold the pleasant goal and call it "good fortune"; do not understand the process, but only perceive the result, and call it "chance."

In all human affairs there are *efforts*, and there are *results*. The strength of the effort is the measure of the result. Change is not. Gifts, powers, material, intellectual, and spiritual possessions are the fruits of effort. They are thoughts completed, objectives accomplished, visions realised.

The vision that you glorify in your mind, the ideal that you enthrone in your heart—this you will build your life by; this you will become.

SERENITY

Calmness of mind is one of the beautiful jewels of wisdom. It is the result of long and patient effort in self-control. Its presence is an indication of ripened experience, and of a more than ordinary knowledge of the laws and operations of thought.

A man becomes calm in the measure that he understands himself as a thought-evolved being. For such knowledge necessitates the understanding of others as the result of thought, and as he develops a right understanding, and sees ever more clearly the internal relations of things by the action of cause and effect, he ceases to fuss, fume, worry, and grieve. He remains poised, steadfast, serene.

The calm man, having learned how to govern himself, knows how to adapt himself to others. And they, in turn reverence his spiritual strength. They feel that they can learn from him and rely upon him. The more tranquil a man becomes, the greater is his success, his influence, his power for good. Even the ordinary trader will find his business prosperity increase as he develops a greater self-control and equanimity, for people will always prefer to deal with a man whose demeanour is equitable.

The strong, calm man is always loved and revered. He is like a shade-giving tree in a thirsty land, or a sheltering rock in a storm. Who does not love a tranquil heart, a sweet-tempered, balanced life? It does not matter whether it rains or shines, or what changes come to those who possess these blessings. For they are always serene and calm. That exquisite poise of character that we call serenity is the last lesson of culture. It is the flowering of life, the fruitage of the soul. It is precious as wisdom—more desirable than fine gold. How insignificant mere money-seeking looks in comparison with a serene life,—a life that dwells in the ocean of truth, beneath the waves, beyond the reach of the tempests, in the Eternal Calm!

"How many people we know who sour their lives, who ruin all that is sweet and beautiful by explosive tempers, who destroy their poise of character and make bad blood! It is a question whether the great majority of people do not ruin their lives and mar their happiness by lack of self-control. How few people we meet in life who are well balanced, who have that exquisite poise which is characteristic of the finished character."

Yes, humanity surges with uncontrolled passion, is tumultuous with ungoverned grief, is blown about by anxiety and doubt. Only the wise man, only he whose thoughts are controlled and purified, makes the winds and the storms of the soul obey him.

Tempest-tossed souls, wherever you may be, under whatever conditions you may live, know this—In the ocean of life the isles of blessedness are smiling and the sunny shore of your ideal awaits your coming. Keep your hands firmly upon the helm of thought. In the core of your soul reclines the commanding Master; He does but sleep; wake Him. Self-control is strength. Right Thought is mastery. Calmness is power.

Say unto your heart, "Peace, be still!"

End

Above Life's Turmoil

FOREWORD

We cannot alter external things, nor shape other people to our liking, nor mould the world to our wishes but we can alter internal things,—our desires, passions, thoughts,—we can shape our liking to other people, and we can mould the inner world of our own mind in accordance with wisdom, and so reconcile it to the outer world of men and things.

The turmoil of the world we cannot avoid, but the disturbances of mind we can overcome. The duties and difficulties of life claim our attention, but we can rise above all anxiety concerning them. Surrounded by noise, we can yet have a quiet mind; involved in responsibilities, the heart can be at rest; in the midst of strife, we can know the abiding peace.

The pieces which comprise this work, unrelated as some of them are in the letter, will be found to be harmonious in the spirit, in that they point the reader towards those heights of self-knowledge and self-conquest which, rising above the turbulence of the world, lift their peaks where the Heavenly Silence reigns.

James Allen

TRUE HAPPINESS

To maintain an unchangeable sweetness of disposition, to think only thoughts that are pure and gentle, and to be happy under all circumstances,—such blessed conditions and such beauty of character and life should be the aim of all, and particularly so of those who wish to lessen the misery of the world. If anyone has failed to lift himself above ungentleness, impurity, and unhappiness, he is greatly deluded if he imagines he can make the world happier by the propagation of any theory or theology. He who is daily living in harshness, impurity, or unhappiness is day by day adding to the sum of the world's misery; whereas he who continually lives in goodwill, and does not depart from happiness, is day by day increasing the sum of the world's happiness, and this independently of any religious beliefs which these may, or may not, hold.

He who has not learned how to be gentle, or giving, loving and happy, has learned very little, great though his book-learning and profound his acquaintance which the letter of Scripture may be, for it is in the process of becoming gentle, pure, and happy that the deep, real and enduring lessons of life are learned. Unbroken sweetness of conduct in the face of all outward antagonism is the infallible indication of a self-conquered soul, the witness of wisdom, and the proof of the possession of Truth.

A sweet and happy soul is the ripened fruit of experience and wisdom, and it sheds abroad the invisible yet powerful aroma of its influence, gladdening the hearts of others, and purifying the world. And all who will, and who have not yet commenced, may begin this day, if they will so resolve, to live sweetly and happily, as becomes the dignity of a true manhood or womanhood. Do not say that your surroundings are against you. A man's surroundings are never against him; they are there to aid him, and all those outward occurrences over which you lose sweetness and peace of mind are the very conditions necessary to your development, and it is only by meeting and overcoming them that you can learn, and grow, and ripen. The fault is in yourself.

Pure happiness is the rightful and healthy condition of the soul, and all may possess it if they will live purely and unselfish.

"Have goodwill
To all that lives, letting unkindness die,
And greed and wrath, so that your lives be made
Like soft airs passing by."

Is this too difficult for you? Then unrest and unhappiness will continue to dwell with you. Your belief and aspiration and resolve are all that are necessary to make it easy, to render it in the near future a thing accomplished, a blessed state realised.

Despondency, irritability, anxiety and complaining, condemning and grumbling—all these are thought-cankers, mind-diseases; they are the indications of a wrong mental condition, and those who suffer therefrom would do well to remedy their thinking and conduct. It is true there is much sin and misery in the world, so that all our love and compassion are needed, but our misery is not needed—there is already too much of that. No, it is our cheerfulness and happiness that are needed for there is too little of that. We can give nothing better to the world than beauty of life and character; without this, all other things are vain; this is pre-eminently excellent; it is enduring, real, and not to be overthrown, and it includes all joy and blessedness.

Cease to dwell pessimistically upon the wrongs around you; dwell no more in complaints about, and revolt against, the evil in others, and commence to live free from all wrong and evil yourself. Peace of mind, pure religion, and true reform lie this way. If you would have others true, be true; if you would have the world emancipated from misery and sin, emancipate yourself; if you would have your home and your surroundings happy, be happy. You can transform everything around you if you will transform yourself.

"Don't bewail and bemoan...
Don't waste yourself in rejection, nor bark against the bad,
but chant the beauties of the good."

And this you will naturally and spontaneously do as you realise the good in yourself.

THE OVERCOMING OF SELF

Many people have very confused and erroneous ideas concerning the terms "the overcoming of self", "the eradication of desire", and "the annihilation of the personality." Some (particularly the intellectual who are prone to theories) regard it as a metaphysical theory altogether apart from life and conduct; while others conclude that it is the crushing out of all life, energy and action, and the attempt to idealise stagnation and death. These errors and confusions, arising as they do in the minds of individuals, can only be removed by the individuals themselves; but perhaps it may make their removal a little less difficult (for those who are seeking Truth) by presenting the matter in another way.

The doctrine of the overcoming or annihilation of self is simplicity itself; indeed, so simple, practical, and close at hand is it that a child of five, whose mind has not yet become clouded with theories, theological schemes and speculative philosophies, would be far more likely to comprehend it than many older people who have lost their hold upon simple and beautiful truths by the adoption of complicated theories.

The annihilation of self consists in weeding out and destroying all those elements in the soul which lead to division, strife, suffering, disease and sorrow. It does not mean the destruction of any good and beautiful and peace-producing quality. For instance, when a man is tempted to irritability or anger, and by a great effort overcomes the selfish tendency, casts it from him, and acts from the spirit of patience and love, in that moment of self-conquest he practices the annihilation of self. Every noble man practices it in part, though he may deny it in his words, and he who carries out this practice to its completion, eradicating every selfish tendency until only the divinely beautiful qualities remain, he is said to have annihilated the personality (all the personal elements) and to have arrived at Truth.

The self which is to be annihilated is composed of the following ten worthless and sorrow-producing elements:

Lust • Hatred • Avarice • Self-indulgence • Self-seeking • Vanity • Pride • Doubt • Dark belief • Delusion

It is the total abandonment, the complete annihilation of these ten elements, for they comprise the body of desire. On the other hand it teaches the cultivation, practice, and preservation of the following ten divine qualities:

Purity • Patience • Humility • Self-sacrifice • Self-reliance • Fearlessness • Knowledge • Wisdom • Compassion • Love

These comprise the Body of Truth, and to live entirely in them is to be a doer and knower of the Truth, is to be an embodiment of Truth. The combination of the ten elements is called Self or the Personality; the combination of the ten qualities produces what is called Truth; the Impersonal; the abiding, real and immortal Man.

It will thus be seen that it is not the destruction of any noble, true, and enduring quality that is taught, but only the destruction of those things that are ignoble, false and evanescent. Neither is this overcoming of self the deprivation of gladness, happiness and joy, but rather is it the constant possession of these things by living in the joy-begetting qualities. It is the abandonment of the lust for enjoyment, but not of enjoyment itself; the destruction of the thirst for pleasure, but not of pleasure itself; the annihilation of the selfish longing for love, and power, and possessions themselves. It is the preservation of all those things which draw and bind men together in unity and concord, and, far from idealising stagnation and death, urges men to the practice of those qualities which lead to the highest, noblest, most effective, and enduring action. He whose actions proceed from some or all of the ten elements wastes his energies upon negations, and does not preserve his soul; but he whose actions proceed from some or all of the ten qualities, he truly and wisely acts and so preserves his soul.

He who lives largely in the ten earthly elements, and who is blind and deaf to the spiritual verities, will find no attraction in the doctrine of self-surrender, for it will appear to him as the complete extinction of his being; but he who is endeavouring to live in the ten heavenly qualities will see the glory and beauty of the doctrine, and will know it as the foundation of Life Eternal. He will also see that when men apprehend and practice it, industry, commerce, government, and every worldly activity will be purified; and action, purpose and intelligence, instead of being destroyed, will be intensified and enlarged, but freed from strife and pain.

THE IMMORTAL MAN

Immortality is here and now, and is not a speculative something beyond the grave. It is a lucid state of consciousness in which the sensations of the body, the varying and unrestful states of mind, and the circumstances and events of life are seen to be of a fleeting and therefore of an illusory character.

Immortality does not belong to time, and will never be found in time; it belongs to Eternity; and just as time is here and now, so is Eternity here and now, and a man may find that Eternity and establish in it, if he will overcome the self that derives its life from the unsatisfying and perishable things of time.

Whilst a man remains immersed in sensation, desire, and the passing events of his day-by-day existence, and regards those sensations, desires, and passing events as of the essence of himself, he can have no knowledge of immortality. The thing which such a man desires, and which he mistakes for immortality, is persistence; that is, a continuous succession of sensations and events in time. Living in, loving and clinging to, the things which stimulate and minister to his immediate gratification, and realising no state of consciousness above and independent of this, he thirsts for its continuance, and strives to banish the thought that he will at last have to part from those earthly luxuries and delights to which he has become enslaved, and which he regards as being inseparable from himself.

Persistence is the antithesis of immortality; and to be absorbed in it is spiritual death. Its very nature is change, impermanence. It is a continual living and dying.

The death of the body can never bestow upon a man immortality. Spirits are not different from men, and live their little feverish life of broken consciousness, and are still immersed in change and mortality. The mortal man, he who thirsts for the persistence of his pleasure-loving personality is still mortal after death, and only lives another life with a beginning and an end without memory of the past, or knowledge of the future.

The immortal man is he who has detached himself from the things of time by having ascended into that state of consciousness which is fixed and unvariable, and is not affected by passing events and sensations. Human life consists of an evermoving procession of events, and in this procession the mortal man is immersed, and he is carried along with it; and being so carried along, he has no knowledge of what is behind and before him. The immortal man is he who has stepped out of this procession, and he stands by unmoved and watches it; and from his fixed place he sees both the before, the behind and the middle of the moving thing called Life. No longer identifying himself with the sensations and fluctuations of the personality, or with the outward changes which make up the life in time, he has become the passionless spectator of his own destiny and of the destinies of the men and nations.

The mortal man, also, is one who is caught in a dream, and he neither knows that he was formerly awake, nor that he will wake again; he is a dreamer without knowledge, nothing more. The immortal man is as one who has awakened out of his dream, and he knows that his dream was not an enduring reality, but a passing illusion. He is a man with knowledge, the knowledge of both states—that of persistence, and that of immortality—and is in full possession of himself.

The mortal man lives in the time or world state of consciousness which begins and ends; the immortal man lives in the cosmic or heaven state of consciousness, in which there is neither beginning nor end, but an eternal now. Such a man remains poised and steadfast under all changes, and the death of his body will not in any way interrupt the eternal consciousness in which he abides. Of such a one it is said, "He shall not taste of death", because he has stepped out of the stream of mortality, and established himself in the abode of Truth. Bodies, personalities, nations, and worlds pass away, but Truth remains, and its glory is undimmed by time. The immortal man, then, is he who has conquered himself; who no longer identifies himself with the self-seeking forces of the personality, but who has trained himself to direct those forces with the hand of a master, and so has brought them into harmony with the causal energy and source of all things.

The fret and fever of life has ceased, doubt and fear are cast out, and death is not for him who has realised the fadeless splendour of that life of Truth by adjusting heart and mind to the eternal and unchangeable verities.

THE USE OF TEMPTATION

The soul, in its journey towards perfection, passes through three distinct stages. The first is the animal stage, in which the man is content to live, in the gratification of his senses, unawakened to the knowledge of sin, or of his divine inheritance, and altogether unconscious of the spiritual possibilities within himself.

The second is the dual stage, in which the mind is continually oscillating between its animal and divine tendencies having become awakened to the consciousness of both. It is during this stage that temptation plays its part in the progress of the soul. It is a stage of continual fighting, of falling and rising, of sinning and repenting, for the man, still loving, and reluctant to leave the gratifications in which he has so long lived, yet also aspires to the purity and excellence of the spiritual state, and he is continually mortified by an undecided choice.

Urged on by the divine life within him, this stage becomes at last one of deep anguish and suffering, and then the soul is ushered into the third stage, that of knowledge, in which the man rises above both sin and temptation, and enters into peace.

Temptation, like contentment in sin, is not a lasting condition, as the majority of people suppose; it is a passing phase, an experience through which the soul must pass; but as to whether a man will pass through that condition in this present life, and realise holiness and heavenly rest here and now, will depend entirely upon the strength of his intellectual and spiritual exertions, and upon the intensity and ardour with which he searches for Truth.

Temptation, with all its attendant torments can be overcome here and now, but it can only be overcome by knowledge. It is a condition of darkness or of semi-darkness. The fully enlightened soul is proof against all temptation. When a man fully understands the source, nature, and meaning of temptation, in that hour he will conquer it, and will rest from his long travail; but whilst he remains in ignorance, attention to religious observances, and much praying and reading of Scripture will fail to bring him peace.

If a man goes out to conquer an enemy, knowing nothing of his enemy's strength, tactics, or place of ambush, he will not only ignominiously fail, but will speedily fall into the hands of the enemy. He who would overcome his enemy the tempter, must discover his stronghold and place of concealment, and must also find out the unguarded gates in his own fortress where his enemy effects so easy an entrance. This necessitates continual meditation, ceaseless watchfulness, and constant and rigid introspection which lays bare, before the spiritual eyes of the tempted one, the vain and selfish motives of his soul. This is the holy warfare of the saints; it is the fight upon which every soul enters when it awakens out of its long sleep of animal indulgence.

Men fail to conquer, and the fight is indefinitely prolonged, because they labour, almost universally, under two delusions: first, that all temptations come from without; and second, that they are tempted because of their goodness. Whilst a man is held in bondage by these two delusions, he will make no progress; when he has shaken them off, he will pass on rapidly from victory to victory, and will taste of spiritual joy and rest.

Two searching truths must take the place of these two delusions, and those truths are: first, that all temptation comes from within; and second, that a man is tempted because of the evil that is within him. The idea that God, a devil, evil spirits, or outward objects are the source of temptation must be dispelled.

The source and cause of all temptation is in the inward desire; that being purified or eliminated, outward objects and extraneous powers are utterly powerless to move the soul to sin or to temptation. The outward object is merely the occasion of the temptation, never the cause; this is in the desire of the one tempted. If the cause existed in the object, all men would be tempted alike, temptation could never be overcome, and men would be hopelessly doomed to endless torment; but seated, as it is, in his own desires, he has the remedy in his own hands, and can become victorious over all temptation by purifying those desires. A man is tempted because there are within him certain desires or states of mind which he has come to regard as unholy. These desires may lie asleep for a long time, and the man may think that he has got rid of them, when suddenly, on the presentation of an outward object, the sleeping desire wakes up and thirsts of immediate gratification; and this is the state of temptation.

The good in a man is never tempted. Goodness destroys temptation. It is the evil in a man that is aroused and tempted. The measure of a man's temptations is the exact register of his own unholiness. As a man purifies his heart, temptation ceases, for when a certain unlawful desire has been taken out of the heart, the object which formerly appealed to it can no longer do so, but becomes dead and powerless, for there is nothing left in the heart that can respond to it. The honest man cannot be tempted to steal, let the occasion be ever so opportune; the man of purified appetites cannot be tempted to gluttony and drunkenness, though the viands and wines be the most luscious; he of an enlightened understanding, whose mind is calm in the strength of inward virtue, can never be tempted to anger, irritability or revenge, and the wiles and charms of the wanton fall upon the purified heart as empty meaningless shadows.

Temptation shows a man just where he is sinful and ignorant, and is a means of urging him on to higher attitudes of knowledge and purity. Without temptation the soul cannot grow and become strong, there could be no wisdom, no real virtue; and though there would be lethargy and death, there could be no peace and no fullness of life. When temptation is understood and conquered, perfection is assured, and such perfection may become any man's who is willing to cast every selfish and impure desire by which he is possessed, into the sacrificial fire of knowledge. Let men, therefore, search diligently for Truth, realising that whilst they are subject to temptation, they have not comprehended Truth, and have much to learn.

You who are tempted know, then, that you are tempted of yourselves. "For every man is tempted when he is drawn away of his own lusts," says the Apostle James. You are tempted because you are clinging to the animal within you and are unwilling to let go; because you are living in the false mortal self which is ever devoid of all true knowledge, knowing nothing, seeking nothing, but its own immediate gratification, ignorant of every Truth, and of every divine Principle. Clinging to that self, you continually suffer the pains of three separate torments; the torment of desire, the torment of repletion, and the torment of remorse.

> *"So flameth Trishna, lust and thirst of things.*
> *Eager, ye cleave to shadows, dote on dreams;*
> *A false self in the midst ye plant, and make*
> *A World around which seems;*
> *Blind to the height beyond; deaf to the sound*
> *Of sweet airs breathed from far past Indra's sky;*
> *Dumb to the summons of the true life kept*
> *For him who false puts by,*
> *So grow the strifes and lusts which make earth's war,*
> *So grieve poor cheated hearts and flow salt tears;*
> *So wax the passions, envies, angers, hates;*
> *So years chase blood-stained years*
> *With wild red feet."*

In that false self lies the germ of every suffering, the blight of every hope, the substance of every grief. When you are ready to give it up; when you are willing to have laid bare before you all its selfishness, impurity, and ignorance, and to confess its darkness to the uttermost, then will you enter upon the life of self-knowledge and self-mastery; you will become conscious of the god within you, of that divine nature which, seeking no gratification, abides in a region of perpetual joy and peace where suffering cannot come and where temptation can find no foothold. Establishing yourself, day by day, more and more firmly in that inward Divinity, the time will at last come when you will be able to say with Him whom millions worship, few understand and fewer still follow, —"The Prince of this world cometh and hath nothing in me."

THE MAN OF INTEGRITY

There are times in the life of every man who takes his stand on high moral principles when his faith in, and knowledge of, those principles is tested to the uttermost, and the way in which he comes out of the fiery trial decides as to whether he has sufficient strength to live as a man of Truth, and join the company of the free, or shall still remain a slave and a hireling to the cruel taskmaster, Self.

Such times of trial generally assume the form of a temptation to do a wrong thing and continue in comfort and prosperity, or to stand by what is right and accept poverty and failure; and so powerful is the trial that, to the tempted one, it plainly appears on the face of things as though, if he chooses the wrong, his material success will be assured for the remainder of his life, but if he does what is right, he will be ruined forever.

Frequently the man at once quails and gives way before this appaling prospect which the Path of Righteousness seems to hold out for him, but should he prove sufficiently strong to withstand this onslaught of temptation, then the inward seducer the spirit of self, assumes the grab of an Angel of Light, and whispers, "Think of your wife and children; think of those who are dependent upon you; will you bring them down to disgrace and starvation?"

Strong indeed and pure must be the man who can come triumphant out of such a trial, but he who does so, enters at once a higher realm of life, where his spiritual eyes are opened to see beautiful things; and then poverty and ruin which seemed inevitable do not come, but a more abiding success comes, and a peaceful heart and a quiet conscience. But he who fails does not obtain the promised prosperity, and his heart is restless and his conscience troubled.

The right-doer cannot ultimately fail, the wrong-doer cannot ultimately succeed, for "Such is the Law which moves to Righteousness which none at last can turn aside or stay," and it is because justice is at the heart of things— because the Great Law is good—that the man of integrity is superior to fear, and failure, and poverty, and shame, and disgrace.As the poet further says of this Law:

> *"The heart of its Love, the end of it*
> *Is peace and consummation sweet-obey."*

The man who fearing the loss of present pleasures or material comforts, denies the Truth within him, can be injured, and robbed, and degraded, and trampled upon, because he has first injured, robbed and degraded, and trampled upon his own nobler self; but the man of steadfast virtue, of unblemished integrity, cannot be subject to such conditions, because he has denied the craven self within him and has taken refuge in Truth. It is not the scourge and the chains which make a man a slave, but the fact that he is a slave.

Slander, Accusation, and malice cannot affect the righteous man, nor call from him any bitter response, nor does he need to go about to defend himself and prove his innocence. His innocence and integrity alone are a sufficient answer to all that hatred may attempt against him. Nor can he ever be subdued by the forces of darkness, having subdued all those forces within himself; but he turns all evil things to good account—out of darkness he brings light, out of hatred love, out of dishonour honour; and slanders, envies, and misrepresentations only serve to make more bright the jewel of Truth within him, and to glorify his high and holy destiny.

Let the man of integrity rejoice and be glad when he is severely tried; let him be thankful that he has been given an opportunity of proving his loyalty to the noble principles which he has espoused; and let him think: "Now is the hour of holy opportunity! Now is the day of triumph for Truth! Though I lose the whole world I will note desert the right!" So thinking, he will return good for evil, and will think compassionately of the wrong-doer.

The slanderer, the backbiter, and the wrong-doer may seem to succeed for a time, but the Law of Justice prevails; the man of integrity may seem to fail for a time, but he is invincible, and in none of the worlds, visible or invisible, can there be forged a weapon that shall prevail against him.

DISCRIMINATION

There is one quality which is pre-eminently necessary to spiritual development, the quality of discrimination.

A man's spiritual progress will be painfully slow and uncertain until there opens with him the eye of discrimination, for without this testing, proving, searching quality, he will but grope in the dark, will be unable to distinguish the real from the unreal, the shadow from the substance, and will so confuse the false with the true as to mistake the inward promptings of his animal nature for those of the spirit of Truth.

A blind man left in a strange place may go grope his way in darkness, but not without much confusion and many painful falls and bruisings. Without discrimination a man is mentally blind, and his life is a painful groping in darkness, a confusion in which vice and virtue are indistinguishable one from the other, where facts are confounded with truths; opinions with principles, and where ideas, events, men, and things appear to be out of all relation to each other.

A man's mind and life should be free from confusion. He should be prepared to meet every mental, material and spiritual difficulty, and should not be inextricably caught (as many are) in the meshes of doubt, indecision and uncertainty when troubles and so-called misfortunes come along. He should be fortified against every emergency that can come against him; but such mental preparedness and strength cannot be attained in any degree without discrimination, and discrimination can only be developed by bringing into play and constantly exercising the analytical faculty.

Mind, like muscle, is developed by use, and the assiduous exercise of the mind in any given direction will develop, in that direction, mental capacity and power. The merely critical faculty is developed and strengthened by continuously comparing and analysing the ideas and opinions of others. But discrimination is something more and greater than criticism; it is a spiritual quality from which the cruelty and egotism which so ,requently accompany criticism are eliminated, and by virtue of which a man sees things as they are, and not as he would like them to be.

Discrimination, being a spiritual quality, can only be developed by spiritual methods, namely, by questioning, examining, and analysing one's own ideas, opinions, and conduct. The critical, fault finding faculty must be withdrawn from its merciless application to the opinions and conduct of others, and must be applied, with undiminished severity, to oneself. A man must be prepared to question his every·opinion, his every thought, and his every line of conduct, and rigorously and logically test them; only in this way can the discrimination which destroys confusion will be developed.

Before a man can enter upon such mental exercise, he must make himself of a teachable spirit. This does not mean that he must allow himself to be led by others; it means that he must be prepared to yield up any cherished thoughts to which he clings, if it will not bear the penetrating light of reason, if it shrivels up before the pure flames of searching aspirations. The man who says, "I am right!" and who refuses to question his position in order to discover whether he is right, will continue to follow the line of his passions and prejudices, and will not acquire discrimination. The man who humbly asks, "Am I right?" and then proceeds to test and prove his position by earnest thought and the love of Truth, will always be able to discover the true and to distinguish it from the false, and he will acquire the priceless possession of discrimination.

The man who is afraid to think searchingly upon his opinions, and to reason critically upon his position, will have to develop moral courage before he can acquire discrimination.

A man must be true to himself, fearless with himself, before he can perceive the Pure Principles of Truth, before he can receive the all-revealing Light of Truth.

The more Truth is inquired of, the brighter it shines; it cannot suffer under examination and analysis.

The more error is questioned, the darker it grows; it cannot survive the entrance of pure and searching thought.

To "prove all things" is to find the good and throw the evil.

He who reasons and meditates learns to discriminate; he who discriminates discovers the eternally True.

Confusion, suffering and spiritual darkness follow the thoughtless.

Harmony, blessedness and the Light of Truth attend upon the thoughtful.

Passion and prejudice are blind, and cannot discriminate: they are still crucifying the Christ and releasing Barabbas.

BELIEF, THE BASIS OF ACTION

Belief is an important word in the teachings of the wise, and it figures prominently in all religions. According to Jesus, a certain kind of belief is necessary to salvation or regeneration, and Buddha definitely taught that right belief is the first and most essential step in the Way of Truth, as without right belief there cannot be right conduct, and he who has not learned how to rightly govern and conduct himself, has not yet comprehended the simplest rudiments of Truth.

Belief as laid down by the Great Teachers, is not belief in any particular school, philosophy, or religion, but consists of an altitude of mind determining the whole course of one's life. Belief and conduct are, therefore inseparable, for the one determines the other.

Belief is the basis of all action, and, this being so, the belief which dominates the hearts or mind is shown in the life. Every man acts, thinks, lives in exact accordance with the belief which is rooted in his innermost being, and such is the mathematical nature of the laws which govern mind that it is absolutely impossible for anyone to believe in two opposing conditions at the same time. For instance, it is impossible to believe in justice and injustice, hatred and love, peace and strife, self and truth. Every man believes in one or the other of these opposites, never in both, and the daily conduct of every man indicates the nature of his belief. The man who believes in justice, who regards it as an eternal and indestructible Principle, never boils over with righteous indignation, does not grow cynical and pessimistic over the inequalities of life, and remains calm and untroubled through all trials and difficulties. It is impossible for him to act otherwise, for he believes that justice reigns, and that, therefore, all that is called injustice is fleeting and illusory.

The man who is continually getting enraged over the injustice of his fellow men, who talks about himself being badly treated, or who mourns over the lack of justice in the world around him, shows by his conduct, his attitude of mind, that he believes in injustice. However he may protest to the contrary, in his inmost heart he believes that confusion and chaos are dominant in the universe, the result being that he dwells in misery and unrest, and his conduct is faulty.

Again, he who believes in love, in its stability and power, practices it under all circumstances, never deviates from it, and bestows it alike upon enemies as upon friends. He who slanders and condemns, who speaks disparagingly of others, or regards them with contempt, believes not in love, but hatred; all his actions prove it, even though with tongue or pen he may eulogise love.

The believer in peace is known by his peaceful conduct. It is impossible for him to engage in strife. If attacked he does not retaliate, for he has seen the majesty of the angel of peace, and he can no longer pay homage to the demon of strife. The stirrer-up of strife, the lover of argument, he who rushes into self-defence upon any or every provocation, believes in strife, and will have naught to do with peace.

Further, he who believes in Truth renounces himself- that is, he refuses to centre his life in those passions, desires, and characteristics which crave only their own gratification, and by thus renouncing he becomes steadfastly fixed in Truth, and lives a wise, beautiful, and blameless life. The believer in self is known by his daily indulgences, gratifications, and vanities, and by the disappointments, sorrows, and mortifications which he continually suffers.

The believer in Truth does not suffer, for he has given up that self which is the cause of such suffering.

It will be seen by the foregoing that every man believes either in permanent and eternal Principles directing human life towards law and harmony, or in the negation of those Principles, with the resultant chaos in human affairs and in his own life.

Belief in the divine Principles of Justice, Compassion, Love, constitutes the right belief laid down by Buddha as being the basis of right conduct, and also the belief unto salvation as emphasised in the Christian Scriptures, for he who so believes cannot do otherwise than build his whole life upon these Principles, and so purifies his heart, and perfects his life.

Belief in the negation of this divine principle constitutes what is called in all religious unbelief and this unbelief is manifested as a sinful, troubled, and imperfect life.

Where there is Right Belief there is a blameless and perfect life; where there is false belief there is sin, there is sorrow, the mind and life are improperly governed, and there is affliction and unrest. "By their fruits ye shall know them."

There is much talk about, "belief in Jesus," but what does belief in Jesus mean? It means belief in his words, in the Principles he enunciated—and lived, in his commandments and in his exemplary life of perfection. He who declares belief in Jesus, and yet is all the time living in his lusts and indulgences, or in the spirit of hatred and condemnation, is self deceived. He believes not in Jesus. He believes in his own animal self. As a faithful servant delights in carrying out the commands of his master, so he who believes in Jesus carries out his commandments, and so is saved from sin. The supreme test of belief in Jesus is this: Do I keep his commandments? And this test is applied by St. John himself in the following words: "He that saith. I know him (Jesus), and keepeth not His Commandments, is a liar, and the truth is not in him. But whoso keepeth his word, in him verily is the word of God perfected."

It will be found after a rigid and impartial analysis, that belief lies at the root of all human conduct. Every thought, every act, every habit, is the direct outcome of a certain fixed belief, and one's conduct alters only as one's belief are modified. What we cling to, in that we believe; what we practice, in that we believe. When our belief in a thing ceases, we can no longer cling to or practice it; it falls away from us as a garment out-worn. Men cling to their lusts, and lies, and vanities, because they believe in them, believe there is gain and happiness in them. When they transfer their belief to the divine qualities of purity and humility, those sins trouble them no more.

Men are saved from error by belief in the supremacy of Truth. They are saved from sin by belief in Holiness or Perfection. They are saved from evil by belief in Good, for every belief is manifested in the life. It is not necessary to inquire as to a man's theological belief, for that is of little or no account, for what can it avail a man to believe that Jesus died for him, or that Jesus is God, or that he is "justified by faith," if he continues to live in his lower, sinful nature? All that is necessary to ask is this: "How does a man live?" "How does he conduct himself under trying circumstances?" The answer to these questions will show whether a man believes in the power of evil or in the power of Good.

He who believes in the power of Good, lives a good, spiritual, or godly life, for Goodness is God, yea, verily is God Himself, and he will soon leave behind him all sins and sorrows who believes, with steadfast and unwavering faith, in the Supreme Good.

THOUGHT AND ACTION

As the fruit to the tree and the water to the spring, so is action to thought. It does not come into manifestation suddenly and without a cause. It is the result of a long and silent growth; the end of a hidden process which has long been gathering force. The fruit of the tree and the water gushing from the rock are both the effect of a combination of natural processes in air and earth which have long worked together in secret to produce the phenomenon; and the beautiful acts of enlightenment and the dark deeds of sin are both the ripened effects of trains of thought which have long been harboured in the mind.

The sudden falling, when greatly tempted, into some grievous sin by one who was believed, and who probably believed himself, to stand firm, is seen neither to be a sudden nor a causeless thing when the hidden process of thought which led up to it are revealed. The falling was merely the end, the outworking, the finished result of what commenced in the mind probably years before. The man had allowed a wrong thought to enter his mind; and a second and a third time he had welcomed it, and allowed it to nestle in his heart. Gradually he became accustomed to it, and cherished, and fondled, and tended it; and so it grew, until at last it attained such strength and force that it attracted to itself the opportunity which enabled it to burst forth and ripen into act. As falls the stately building whose foundations have been gradually undermined by the action of water, so at last falls the strong man who allows corrupt thoughts to creep into his mind and secretly undermine his character.

When it is seen that all sin and temptation are the natural outcome of the thoughts of the individual, the way to overcome sin and temptation becomes plain, and its achievement a near possibility, and, sooner or later, a certain reality; for if a man will admit, cherish, and brood upon thoughts that are pure and good, those thoughts, just as surely as the impure, will grow and gather force, and will at last attract to themselves the opportunities which will enable them to ripen into act.

"There is nothing hidden that shall not be revealed," and every thought that is harboured in the mind must, by virtue of the impelling force which is inherent in the universe, at last blossom into act good or bad according to its nature. The divine Teacher and the sensualist are both the product of their own thoughts, and have become what they are as the result of the seeds of thought which they have implanted, are allowed to fall, into the garden of the heart, and have afterwards watered, tended, and cultivated.

Let no man think he can overcome sin and temptation by wrestling with opportunity; he can only overcome them by purifying his thoughts; and if he will, day by day, in the silence of his soul, and in the performance of his duties, strenuously overcome all erroneous inclination, and put in its place thoughts that are true and that will endure the light, opportunity to do evil will give place to opportunity for accomplishing good, for a man can only attract that to him which is in harmony with his nature, and no temptation can gravitate to a man unless there is that in his heart which is capable of responding to it.

Guard well your thoughts, reader, for what you really are in your secret thoughts today, be it good or evil, you will, sooner or later, become in actual deed. He who unwearingly guards the portals of his mind against the intrusion of sinful thoughts, and occupies himself with loving thoughts, with pure, strong, and beautiful thoughts, will, when the season of their ripening comes, bringforth the fruits of gentle and holy deeds, and no temptation that can come against him shall find him unarmed or unprepared.

YOUR MENTAL ATTITUDE

As a being of thought, your dominant mental attitude will determine your condition in life. It will also be the gauge of your knowledge and the measures of your attainment. The so-called limitations of your nature are the boundary lines of your thoughts; they are self-erected fences, and can be drawn to a narrower circle, extended to a wider, or be allowed to remain.

You are the thinker of your thoughts and as such you are the maker of yourself and condition. Thought is causal and creative, and appears in your character and life in the form of results. There are no accidents in your life. Both its harmonies and antagonisms are the responsive echoes of your thoughts. A man thinks, and his life appears.

If your dominant mental attitude is peaceable and lovable, bliss and blessedness will follow you; if it be resistant and hateful, trouble and distress will cloud your pathway. Out of ill-will will come grief and disaster; out of good-will, healing and reparation.

You imagine your circumstances as being separate from yourself, but they are intimately related to your thought world. Nothing appears without an adequate cause. Everything that happens is just. Nothing is fated, everything is formed.

As you think, you travel; as you love, you attract. You are today where your thoughts have brought you; you will be tomorrow where your thoughts take you. You cannot escape the result of your thoughts, but you can endure and learn, can accept and be glad.

You will always come to the place where your love (your most abiding and intense thought) can receive its measure of gratification. If your love be base, you will come to a base place; if it be beautiful, you will come to a beautiful place.

You can alter your thoughts, and so alter your condition. Strive to perceive the vastness and grandeur of your responsibility. You are powerful, not powerless. You are as powerful to obey as you are to disobey; as strong to be pure as to be impure; as ready for wisdom as for ignorance. You can learn what you will, can remain as ignorant as you choose. If you love knowledge you will obtain it; if you love wisdom you will secure it; if you love purity you will realise it. All things await your acceptance, and you choose by the thoughts which you entertain.

A man remains ignorant because he loves ignorance, and chooses ignorant thoughts; a man becomes wise because he loves wisdom and chooses wise thoughts. No man is hindered by another; he is only hindered by himself. No man suffers because of another; he suffers only because of himself. By the noble Gateway of Pure Thought you can enter the highest Heaven; by the ignoble doorway of impure thought you can descend into the lowest hell.

Your mental attitude towards others will faithfully react upon yourself, and will manifest itself in every relation of your life. Every impure and selfish thought that you send out comes back to you in your circumstances in some form of suffering; every pure and unselfish thought returns to you in some form of blessedness. Your circumstances are effects of which the cause is inward and invisible. As the father-mother of your thoughts you are the maker of your state and condition. When you know yourself, you will perceive, that every event in your life is weighed in the faultless balance of equity. When you understand the law within your mind you will cease to regard yourself as the impotent and blind tool of circumstances, and will become the strong and seeing master.

SOWING AND REAPING

Go into the fields and country lanes in the spring-time, and you will see farmers and gardeners busy sowing seeds in the newly prepared soil. If you were to ask any one of those gardeners or farmers what kind of produce he expected from the seed he was sowing, he would doubtless regard you as foolish, and would tell you that he does not "expect" at all, that it is a matter of common knowledge that his produce will be of the kind which he is sowing, and that he is sowing wheat, or barley, or turnips, as the case may be, in order to reproduce that particular kind.

Every fact and process in Nature contains a moral lesson for the wise man. There is no law in the world of Nature around us which is not to be found operating with the same mathematical certainty in the mind of man and in human life. All the parables of Jesus are illustrative of this truth, and are drawn from the simple facts of Nature. There is a process of seed-sowing in the mind and life a spiritual sowing which leads to a harvest according to the kind of seed sown. Thoughts, words, and acts are seeds sown, and, by the inviolable law of things, they produce after their kind.

The man who thinks hateful thoughts brings hatred upon himself. The man who thinks loving thoughts is loved. The man whose thoughts, words and acts are sincere, is surrounded by sincere friends; the insincere man is surrounded by insincere friends. The man who sows wrong thoughts and deeds, and prays that God will bless him, is in the position of a farmer who, having sown weeds, asks God to bring forth for him a harvest of wheat.

> *"That which ye sow, ye reap; see yonder fields*
> *The sesamum was sesamum, the corn*
> *Was corn; the silence and the darkness knew;*
> *So is a man's fate born."*
> *"He cometh reaper of the things he sowed."*

He who would be blest, let him scatter blessings. He who would be happy, let him consider the happiness of others.

Then there is another side to this seed sowing. The farmer must scatter all his seed upon the land, and then leave it to the elements. Were he to covetously hoard his seed, he would lose both it and his produce, for his seed would perish. It perishes when he sows it, but in perishing it brings forth a great abundance. So in life, we get by giving; we grow rich by scattering. The man who says he is in possession of knowledge which he cannot give out because the world is incapable of receiving it, either does not possess such knowledge, or, if he does, will soon be deprived of it—if he is not already so deprived. To hoard is to lose; to exclusively retain is to be dispossessed.

Even the man who would increase his material wealth must be willing to part with (invest) what little capital he has, and then wait for the increase. So long as he retains his hold on his precious money, he will not only remain poor, but will be growing poorer everyday. He will, after all, lose the thing he loves, and will lose it without increase. But if he wisely lets it go; if, like the farmer, he scatters his seeds of gold, then he can faithfully wait for, and reasonably expect, the increase.

Men are asking God to give them peace and purity, and righteousness and blessedness, but are not obtaining these things; and why not? Because they are not practising them, not sowing them. I once heard a preacher pray very earnestly for forgiveness, and shortly afterwards, in the course of his sermon, he called upon his congregation to "show no mercy to the enemies of the church." Such self-delusion is pitiful, and men have yet to learn that the way to obtain peace and blessedness is to scatter peaceful and blessed thoughts, words, and deeds.

Men believe that they can sow the seeds of strife, impurity, and unbrotherliness, and then gather in a rich harvest of peace, purity and concord by merely asking for it. What more pathetic sight than to see an irritable and quarrelsome man praying for peace. Men reap that which they sow, and any man can reap all blessedness now and at once, if he will put aside selfishness, and sow broadcast the seeds of kindness, gentleness, and love.

If a man is troubled, perplexed, sorrowful, or unhappy, let him ask:
"What mental seeds have I been sowing?"
"What seeds am I sowing?"
"What have I done for others?"
"What is my attitude towards others?"
"What seeds of trouble and sorrow and unhappiness have I sown
that I should thus reap these bitter weeds?"

Let him seek within and find, and having found, let him abandon all the seeds of self, and sow, henceforth, only the seeds of

Truth. Let him learn of the farmer the simple truths of wisdom.

THE REIGN OF LAW

The little party gods have had their day. The arbitrary gods, creatures of human caprice and ignorance, are falling into disrepute. Men have quarrelled over and defended them until they have grown weary of the strife, and now, everywhere, they are relinquishing and breaking up these helpless idols of their long worship.

The god of revenge, hatred and jealousy, who gloats over the downfall of his enemies; the partial god who gratifies all our narrow and selfish desires; the god who saves only the creatures of his particular special creed; the god of exclusiveness and favouritism; such were the gods (miscalled by us God) of our soul's infancy, gods base and foolish as ourselves, the fabrications of our selfish self. And we relinquished our petty gods with bitter tears and misgivings, and broke our idols with bleeding hands. But in so doing we did not lose sight of God; nay we drew nearer to the great, silent Heart of Love. Destroying the idols of self, we began to comprehend somewhat of the Power which cannot be destroyed, and entered into a wider knowledge of the God of Love, of Peace, of Joy; the God in whom revenge and partiality cannot exist; the God of Light, from whose presence the darkness of fear and doubt and selfishness cannot choose but flee.

We have reached one of those epochs in the world's progress which witnesses the passing of the false gods; the gods of human selfishness and human illusion. The new-old revelation of one universal impersonal Truth has again dawned upon the world, and its searching light has carried consternation to the perishable gods who take shelter under the shadow of self.

Men have lost faith in a god who can be cajoled, who rules arbitrarily and capriciously, subverting the whole order of things to gratify the wishes of his worshippers, and are turning, with a new light in their eyes and a new joy in their hearts, to the God of Law.

And to Him they turn, not for personal happiness and gratification, but for knowledge, for understanding, for wisdom, for liberation from the bondage of self. And thus turning, they do not seek in vain, nor are they sent away empty and discomfited. They find within themselves the reign of Law, that every thought, every impulse, every act and word brings about a result in exact accordance with its own nature; that thoughts of love bring about beautiful and blissful conditions, that hateful thoughts bring about distorted and painful conditions, that thoughts and acts good and evil are weighed in the faultless balance of the Supreme Law, and receive their equal measure of blessedness on the one hand, and misery on the other. And thus finding they enter a new Path, the Path of Obedience to the Law. Entering that Path they no longer accuse, no longer doubt, no longer fret and despond, for they know that God is right, the universal laws are right, the cosmos is right, and that they themselves are wrong, if wrong there is, and that their salvation depends upon themselves, upon their own efforts, upon their personal acceptance of that which is good and deliberate rejection of that which is evil. No longer merely hearers, they become doers of the Word, and they acquire knowledge, they receive understanding, they grow in wisdom, and they enter into the glorious life of liberation from the bondage of self.

"The Law of the Lord is perfect, enlightening the eyes." Imperfection lies in man's ignorance, in man's blind folly. Perfection, which is knowledge of the Perfect Law, is ready for all who earnestly seek it; it belongs to the order of things; it is yours and mine now if we will only put self-seeking on one side, and adopt the life of self-obliteration.

The knowledge of Truth, with its unspeakable joy, its calmness and quiet strength, is not for those who persist in clinging to their "rights," defending their "interests," and fighting for their "opinions"; whose works are imbued with the personal "I," and who build upon the shifting sands of selfishness and egotism. It is for those who renounce these causes of strife, these sources of pain and sorrow; and they are, indeed, Children of Truth, disciples of the Master, worshippers of the most High.

The Children of Truth are in the world today; they are thinking, acting, writing, speaking; yes, even prophets are amongst us, and their influence is pervading the whole earth. An undercurrent of holy joy is gathering force in the world, so that men and women are moved with new aspirations and hopes, and even those who neither see nor hear, feel within themselves strange yearnings after a better and fuller life.

The Law reigns, and it reigns in men's hearts and lives; and they have come to understand the reign of Law who have sought out the Tabernacle of the true God by the fair pathway of unselfishness.

God does not alter for man, for this would mean that the perfect must become imperfect; man must alter for God, and this implies that the imperfect must become perfect. The Law cannot be broken for man, otherwise confusion would ensue; man must obey the Law; this is in accordance with harmony, order, justice.

There is no more painful bondage than to be at the mercy of one's inclinations; no greater liberty than utmost obedience to the Law of Being. And the Law is that the heart shall be purified, the mind regenerated, and the whole being brought in subjection to Love till self is dead and Love is all in all, for the reign of Law is the reign of Love. And Love waits for all , rejecting none. Love may be claimed and entered into now, for it is the heritage of all.

Ah, beautiful Truth! To know that now man may accept his divine heritage, and enter the Kingdom of Heaven!

Oh, pitiful error! To know that man rejects it because of love of self!

Obedience to the Law means the destruction of sin and self, and the realisation of unclouded joy and undying peace.

Clinging to one's selfish inclinations means the drawing about one's soul clouds of pain and sorrow which darken the light of Truth; the shutting out of oneself from all real blessedness; for "whatsoever a man sows that shall he also reap."

Verily the Law reigneth, and reigneth for ever, and Justice and Love are its eternal ministers.

THE SUPREME JUSTICE

The material universe is maintained and preserved by the equilibrium of its forces.

The moral universe is sustained and protected by the perfect balance of its equivalents.

As in the physical world Nature abhors a vacuum, so in the spiritual world disharmony is annulled.

Underlying the disturbances and destructions of Nature, and behind the mutability of its forms, there abides the eternal and perfect mathematical symmetry; and at the heart of life, behind all its pain, uncertainty, and unrest, there abide the eternal harmony, the unbroken peace, and inviolable Justice.

Is there, then, no injustice in the universe? There is injustice, and there is not. It depends upon the kind of life and the state of consciousness from which a man looks out upon the world and judges. The man who lives in his passions sees injustice everywhere; the man who has overcome his passions, sees the operations of Justice in every department of human life. Injustice is the confused, feverish dream of passion, real enough to those who are dreaming it; Justice is the permanent reality in life, gloriously visible to those who have wakened out of the painful nightmare of self.

The Divine Order cannot be perceived until passion and self are transcended; the Faultless Justice cannot be apprehended until all sense of injury and wrong is consumed in the pure flames of all-embracing Love.

The man who thinks, "I have been slighted, I have been injured, I have been insulted, I have been treated unjustly," cannot know what Justice is; blinded by self, he cannot perceive the pure Principles of Truth, and brooding upon his wrongs, he lives in continual misery.

In the region of passion there is a ceaseless conflict of forces causing suffering to all who are involved in them. There is action and reaction, deed and consequence, cause and effect; and within and above all is the Divine Justice regulating the play of forces with the utmost mathematical accuracy, balancing cause and effect with the finest precision. But this Justice is not perceived - cannot be perceived - by those who are engaged in the conflict; before this can be done, the fierce warfare of passion must be left behind.

The world of passion is the abode of schisms, quarrellings, wars, law-suits, accusations, condemnations, impurities, weaknesses, follies, hatreds, revenges, and resentments. How can a man perceive Justice or understand Truth who is even partly involved in the fierce play of its blinding elements? As well expect a man caught in the flames of a burning building to sit down and reason out the cause of the fire.

In this realm of passion, men see injustice in the actions of others because, seeing only immediate appearances, they regard every act as standing by itself, undetached from cause and consequence. Having no knowledge of cause and effect in the moral sphere, men do not see the exacting and balancing process which is momentarily proceeding, nor do they ever regard their own actions as unjust, but only the actions of others. A boy beats a defenceless animal, then a man beats the defenceless boy for his cruelty, then a stronger man attacks the man for his cruelty to the boy. Each believes the other to be unjust and cruel, and himself to be just and humane; and doubtless most of all would the boy justify his conduct toward the animal as altogether necessary. Thus does ignorance keep alive hatred and strife; thus do men blindly inflict suffering upon themselves, living in passion and resentment, and not finding the true way in life. Hatred is met with hatred, passion with passion, strife with strife. The man who kills is himself killed; the thief who lives by depriving others is himself deprived; the beast that preys on others is hunted and killed; the accuser is accused, the condemner is condemned, the denouncer is persecuted.

> *"By this the slayer's knife doth stab himself,*
> *The unjust judge has lost his own defender,*
> *The false tongue dooms its lie, the creeping thief*
> *And spoiler rob to render.*
> *Such is the Law."*

Passion, also has its active and passive sides. Fool and fraud, oppressor and slave, aggressor and retaliator, the charlatan and the superstitious, complement each other, and come together by the operation of the Law of Justice. Men unconsciously cooperate in the mutual production of affliction; "the blind lead the blind, and both fall together into the ditch." Pain, grief, sorrow, and misery are the fruits of which passion is the flower.

Where the passion-bound soul sees only injustice, the good man, he who has conquered passion, sees cause and effect, sees the Supreme Justice. It is impossible for such a man to regard himself as treated unjustly, because he has ceased to see injustice. He knows that no one can injure or cheat him, having ceased to injure or cheat himself. However passionately or ignorantly men may act towards him, it cannot possibly cause him any pain,

56

for he knows that whatever comes to him (it may be abuse and persecution) can only come as the effect of what he himself has formerly sent out. He therefore regards all things as good, rejoices in all things, loves his enemies and blesses them that curse him, regarding them as the blind but beneficent instruments by which he is enabled to pay his moral debts to the Great Law.

The good man, having put away all resentment, retaliation, self-seeking, and egotism, has arrived at a state of equilibrium, and has thereby become identified with the Eternal and Universal Equilibrium. Having lifted himself above the blind forces of passion, he understands those forces, contemplates them with a calm penetrating insight, like the solitary dweller upon a mountain who looks down upon the conflict of the storms beneath his feet. For him, injustice has ceased, and he sees ignorance and suffering on the one hand and enlightenment and bliss on the other. He sees that not only do the fool and the slave need his sympathy, but that the fraud and the oppressor are equally in need of it, and so his compassion is extended towards all.

The Supreme Justice and the Supreme Love are one. Cause and effect cannot be avoided; consequences cannot be escaped.

While a man is given to hatred, resentment, anger and condemnation, he is subject to injustice as the dreamer to his dream, and cannot do otherwise than see injustice; but he who has overcome those fiery and binding elements, knows that unerring Justice presides over all, that in reality there is no such thing as injustice in the whole of the universe.

THE USE OF REASON

We have heard it said that reason is a blind guide, and that it draws men away from Truth rather than leads them to it. If this were true, it were better to remain, or to become, unreasonable, and to persuade others so to do. We have found, however, that the diligent cultivation of the divine faculty of reason brings about calmness and mental poise, and enables one to meet cheerfully the problems and difficulties of life.

It is true there is a higher light than reason; even that of the Spirit of Truth itself, but without the aid of reason, Truth cannot be apprehended. They who refuse to trim the lamp of reason will never, whilst they so refuse, perceive the light of Truth, for the light of reason is a reflection of that Light.

Reason is a purely abstract quality, and comes midway between the animal and divine consciousness in man, and leads, if rightly employed, from the darkness of one to the Light of the other. It is true that reason may be enlisted in the service of the lower, self-seeking nature, but this is only a result of its partial and imperfect exercise. A fuller development of reason leads away from the selfish nature, and ultimately allies the soul with the highest, the divine.

That spiritual perceival who, searching for the Holy Grail of the Perfect Life, is again and again

> *"Left alone,*
> *And wearying in a land of sand and thorns,"*

is not so stranded because he has followed reason, but because he is still clinging to, and is reluctant to leave, some remnants of his lower nature. He who will use the light of reason as a torch to search for Truth will not be left at last in comfortless darkness.

"Come, now, and let us reason together, saith the Lord; though your sins be as scarlet, they shall be as white as snow."

Many men and women pass through untold sufferings, and at last die in their sins, because they refuse to reason; because they cling to those dark delusions which even a faint glimmer of the light of reason would dispel; and all must use their reason freely, fully, and faithfully, who would exchange the scarlet robe of sin and suffering for the white garment of blamelessness and peace.

It is because we have proved and know these truths that we exhort men to

> *"Tread the middle road, whose course*
> *Bright reason traces, and soft quiet smooths,"*

for reason leads away from passion and selfishness into the quiet ways of sweet persuasion and gentle forgiveness, and he will never be led astray, nor will he follow blind guides, who faithfully adheres to the Apostolic injunction, "Prove all things, and hold fast that which is good." They, therefore, who despise the light of reason, despise the Light of Truth.

Large numbers of people are possessed of the strange delusion that reason is somehow intimately connected with the denial of the existence of God. This is probably due to the fact that those who try to prove that there is no God usually profess to take their stand upon reason, while those who try to prove the reverse generally profess to take their stand on faith. Such argumentative combatants, however, are frequently governed more by prejudice than either reason or faith, their object being not to find Truth, but to defend and confirm a preconceived opinion.

Reason is concerned, not with ephemeral opinions, but with the established truth of things, and he who is possessed of the faculty of reason in its purity and excellence can never be enslaved by prejudice, and will put from him all preconceived opinions as worthless. He will neither attempt to prove nor disprove, but after balancing extremes and bringing together all apparent contradictions, he will carefully and dispassionately weigh and consider them, and so arrive at Truth.

Reason is, in reality, associated with all that is pure and gentle, moderate and just. It is said of a violent man that he is "unreasonable," of a kind and considerate man that he is "reasonable," and of an insane man that he has "lost his reason." Thus it is seen that the word is used, even to a great extent unconsciously, though none the less truly, in a very comprehensive sense, and though reason is not actually love and thoughtfulness and gentleness and sanity, it leads to and is intimately connected with these divine qualities, and cannot, except for purposes of analysis, be dissociated from them.

Reason represents all that is high and noble in man. It distinguishes him from the brute which blindly follows its animal inclinations, and just in the degree that man disobeys the voice of reason and follows his inclinations does he become brutish. As Milton says:

> *"Reason in man obscured, or not obeyed,*
> *Immediately inordinate desires*
> *And upstart passions catch the government*
> *From reason, and to servitude reduce*
> *Man till then free."*

The following definition of "reason" from Nuttall's Dictionary will give some idea of the comprehensiveness of the word:

The cause, ground, principle, or motive of anything said or done; efficient cause; final cause; the faculty of intelligence in man; especially the faculty by which we arrive at necessary truth.

It will thus be seen that "reason" is a term, the breadth of which is almost sufficient to embrace even Truth itself, and Archbishop Trench tells us in his celebrated work On the Study of Words that the terms Reason and Word "are indeed so essentially one and the same that the Greek language has one word for them both," so that the Word of God is the Reason of God; and one of the renderings of Lao-tze's "Tao" is Reason, so that in the Chinese translation of our New Testament, St. John's Gospel runs; "In the beginning was the Tao."

To the undeveloped and uncharitable mind all words have narrow applications, but as a man enlarges his sympathies and broadens his intelligence, words become filled with rich meanings and assume comprehensive proportions. Let us therefore cease from foolish quarrellings about words, and, like reasonable beings, search for principles and practice those things which make for unity and peace.

SELF-DISCIPLINE

A man does not live until he begins to discipline himself; he merely exists. Like an animal he gratifies his desires and pursues his inclinations just where they may lead him. He is happy as a beast is happy, because he is not conscious of what he is depriving himself; he suffers as the beast suffers, because he does not know the way out of suffering. He does not intelligently reflect upon life, and lives in a series of sensations, longings, and confused memories which are unrelated to any central idea or principle. A man whose inner life is so ungoverned and chaotic must necessarily manifest this confusion in the visible conditions of his outer life in the world; and though for a time, running with the stream of his desires, he may draw to himself a more or less large share of the outer necessities and comforts of life, he never achieves any real success nor accomplishes any real good, and sooner or later wordly failure and disaster are inevitable, as the direct result of the inward failure to properly adjust and regulate those mental forces which make the outer life.

Before a man accomplish anything of an enduring nature in the world he must first of all acquire some measure of success in the management of his own mind. This is as mathematical a truism as that two and two are four, for, "out of the heart are the issues of life." If a man cannot govern the forces within himself, he cannot hold a firm hand upon the outer activities which form his visible life. On the other hand, as a man succeeds, in governing himself he rises to higher and higher levels of power and usefulness and success in the world.

The only difference between the life of the beast and that of the undisciplined man is that the man has a wider variety of desires, and experiences a greater intensity of suffering. It may be said of such a man that he is dead, being truly dead to self-control, chastity, fortitude, and all the nobler qualities which constitute life. In the consciousness of such a man the crucified Christ lies entombed, awaiting that resurrection which shall revive the mortal sufferer, and wake him up to a knowledge of the realities of his existence.

With the practice of self-discipline a man begins to live, for he then commences to rise above the inward confusion and to adjust his conduct to a steadfast centre within himself. He ceases to follow where inclination leads him, reins in the steed of his desires, and lives in accordance with the dictates of reason and wisdom. Hitherto his life has been without purpose or meaning, but now he begins to consciously mould his own destiny; he is "clothed and in his right mind."

In the process of self-discipline there are three stages namely;

1. Control
2. Purification
3. Relinquishment

A man begins to discipline himself by controlling those passions which have hitherto controlled him; he resists temptation and guards himself against all those tendencies to selfish gratifications which are so easy and natural, and which have formerly dominated him. He brings his appetite into subjection, and begins to eat as a reasonable and responsible being, practising moderation and thoughtfulness in the selection of his food, with the object of making his body a pure instrument through which he may live and act as becomes a man, and no longer degrading that body by pandering to gustatory pleasure. He puts a check upon his tongue, his temper, and, in fact, his every animal desire and tendency, and this he does by referring all his acts to a fixed centre within himself. It is a process of living from within outward, instead of, as formerly, from without inward. He conceives of an ideal, and, enshrining that ideal in the sacred recesses of his heart, he regulates his conduct in accordance with its exaction and demands.

There is a philosophical hypothesis that at the heart of every atom and every aggregation of atoms in the universe there is a motionless centre which is the sustaining source of all the universal activities. Be this as it may, there is certainly in the heart of every man and woman a selfless centre without which the outer man could not be, and the ignoring of which leads to suffering and confusion. This selfless centre which takes the form, in the mind, of an ideal of unselfishness and spotless purity, the attainment of which is desirable, is man's eternal refuge from the storms of passion and all the conflicting elements of his lower nature. It is the Rock of Ages, the Christ within, the divine and immortal in all men.

As a man practices self-control he approximates more and more to this inward reality, and is less and less swayed by passion and grief, pleasure and pain, and lives a steadfast and virtuous life, manifesting manly strength and fortitude. The restraining of the passions, however, is merely the initial stage in self-discipline, and is immediately followed by the process of Purification. By this a man so purifies himself as to take passion out of the heart and mind altogether; not merely restraining it when it rises within him, but preventing it from rising altogether. By merely restraining his passions a man can never arrive at peace, can never actualise his ideal; he must purify those passions.

It is in the purification of his lower nature that a man becomes strong and god-like, standing firmly upon the ideal centre within, and rendering all temptations powerless and ineffectual. This purification is effected by thoughtful care, earnest meditation, and holy aspiration; and as success is achieved confusion of mind and life pass away, and calmness of mind and spiritualised conduct ensure.

True strength and power and usefulness are born of self-purification, for the lower animal forces are not lost, but are transmuted into intellectual and spiritual energy. The pure life (Pure in thought and deed) is a life of conservation of energy; the impure life (even should the impurity not extent beyond thought) is a life of dissipation of energy. The pure man is more capable, and therefore more fit to succeed in his plans and to accomplish his purposes than the impure. Where the impure man fails, the pure man will step in and be victorious, because he directs his energies with a calmer mind and a greater definiteness and strength of purpose.

With the growth in purity; all the elements which constitute a strong and virtuous manhood are developed in an increasing degree of power, and as a man brings his lower nature into subjection, and makes his passions do his bidding, just so much will he mould the outer circumstances of his life, and influence others for good.

The third stage of self-discipline, that of Relinquishment, is a process of letting the lower desires and all impure and unworthy thoughts drop out of the mind, and also refusing to give them any admittance, leaving them to perish. As a man grows purer, he perceives that all evil is powerless, unless it receives his encouragement, and so he ignores it, and lets it pass out of his life. It is by pursuing this aspect of self-discipline that a man enters into and realises the divine life, and manifests those qualities which are distinctly divine, such as wisdom, patience, non-resistance, compassion, and love. It is here, also, where a man becomes consciously immortal, rising above all the fluctuations and uncertainties of life, and living in an intelligent and unchangeable peace.

By self-discipline a man attains to every degree of virtue and holiness, and finally becomes a purified son of God, realising his oneness with the central heart of all things.

Without self-discipline a man drifts lower and lower, approximating more and more nearly to the beast, until at last he grovels, a lost creature, in the mire of his own befoulment. By self-discipline a man rises higher and higher, approximating more and more nearly to the divine, until at last he stands erect in his divine dignity, a saved soul, glorified by the radiance of his purity. Let a man discipline himself, and he will live; let a man cease to discipline himself, and he will perish. As a tree grows in beauty, health, and fruitfulness by being carefully pruned and tended, so a man grows in grace and beauty of life by cutting away all the branches of evil from his mind, and as he tends and develops the good by constant and unfailing effort.

As a man by practice acquires proficiency in his craft, so the earnest man acquires proficiency in goodness and wisdom. Men shrink from self-discipline because in its early stages it is painful and repellent, and the yielding to desire is, at first, sweet and inviting; but the end of desire is darkness and unrest, whereas the fruits of discipline are immortality and peace.

RESOLUTION

Resolution is the directing and impelling force in individual progress. Without it no substantial work can be accomplished. Not until a man brings resolution to bear upon his life does he consciously and rapidly develop, for a life without resolution is a life without aims, and a life without aims is a drifting and unstable thing.

Resolution may of course be linked to downward tendencies, but it is more usually the companion of noble aims and lofty ideals, and I am dealing with it in this its highest use and application.

When a man makes a resolution, it means that he is dissatisfied with his condition, and is commencing to take himself in hand with a view to producing a better piece of workmanship out of the mental materials of which his character and life are composed, and in so far as he is true to his resolution he will succeed in accomplishing his purpose.

The vows of the saintly once were holy resolutions directed toward some victory over self, and the beautiful achievements of holy men and the glorious conquests of the Divine Teachers were rendered possible and actual by the pursuit of unswerving resolution.

To arrive at the fixed determination to walk a higher path than heretofore, although it reveals the great difficulties which have to be surmounted, it yet makes possible the treading of that path, and illuminates its dark places with the golden halo of success.

The true resolution is the crisis of long thought, protracted struggle, or fervent but unsatisfied aspiration. It is no light thing, no whimsical impulse or vague desire, but a solemn and irrevocable determination not to rest nor cease from effort until the high purpose which is held in view is fully accomplished.

Half-hearted and premature resolution is no resolution at all, and is shattered at the first difficulty.

A man should be slow to form a resolution. He should searchingly examine his position and take into consideration every circumstance and difficulty connected with his decision, and should be fully prepared to meet them. He should be sure that he completely understands the nature of his resolution, that his mind is finally made up, and that he is without fear and doubt in the matter. With the mind thus prepared, the resolution that is formed will not be departed from, and by the aid of it a man will, in due time, accomplish his strong purpose.

Hasty resolutions are futile.

The mind must be fortified to endure.

Immediately the resolution to walk a higher path is made, temptation and trial begin. Men have found that no sooner have they decided to lead a truer and nobler life than they have been overwhelmed with such a torrent of new temptations and difficulties as make their position almost unendurable, and many men, because of this, relinquish their resolution.

But these temptations and trials are a necessary part of the work of regeneration upon which the man has decided and must be hailed as friends and met with courage if the resolution is to do its work. For what is the real nature of a resolution? Is it not the sudden checking of a particular stream of conduct, and the endeavour to open up an entirely new channel? Think of an engineer who decides to turn the course of a powerfully running stream or river in another direction. He must first cut his new channel, and must take every precaution to avoid failure in the carrying out of his undertaking. But when he comes to the all-important task of directing the stream into its new channel, then the flowing force, which for ages has steadily pursued its accustomed course, becomes refractory, and all the patience and care and skill of the engineer will be required for the successful completion of the work. It is even so with the man who determines to turn his course of conduct in another and higher direction. Having prepared his mind, which is the cutting of a new channel, he then proceeds to the work of redirecting his mental forces—which have hitherto flowed on uninterruptedly—into the new course. Immediately this is attempted, the arrested energy begins to assert itself in the form of powerful temptations and trials hitherto unknown and unencountered. And this is exactly as it should be; it is the law; and the same law that is in the water is in the mind. No man can improve upon the established law of things, but he can learn to understand the law instead of complaining, and wishing things were different. The man who understands all that is involved in the regeneration of his mind will "glory in tribulations," knowing that only by passing through them can he gain strength, obtain purity of heart, and arrive at peace. And as the engineer at last (perhaps after many mistakes and failures) succeeds in getting the stream to flow on peacefully in the broader and better channel, and the turbulence of the water is spent, and all dams can be removed, so the man of resolution at last succeeds in directing his thoughts and acts into the better and nobler way to which he aspires, and temptations and trials give place to steadfast strength and settled peace.

He whose life is not in harmony with his conscience and who is anxious to remedy his mind and conduct in a particular direction, let him first mature his purpose by earnest thought and self-examination, and having arrived at a final conclusion, let him frame his resolution, and having done so let him not swerve from it, let him remain true to his decision under all circumstances, and he cannot fail to achieve his good purpose; for the Great Law ever shields and protects him who, no matter how deep his sins, or how great and many his failures and mistakes, has, deep in his heart, resolved upon the finding of a better way, and every obstacle must at last give way before a matured and unshaken resolution.

THE GLORIOUS CONQUEST

Truth can only be apprehended by the conquest of self.

Blessedness can only be arrived at by overcoming the lower nature.

The way of Truth is barred by a man's self.

The only enemies that can actually hinder him are his own passions and delusions.

Until a man realises this, and commences to cleanse his heart, he has not found the Path which leads to knowledge and peace.

Until passion is transcended, Truth remains unknown. This is the Divine Law.

A man cannot keep his passions and have Truth as well.

Error is not slain until selfishness is dead.

The overcoming of self is no mystical theory, but a very real and practical thing.

It is a process which must be pursued daily and hourly, with unswerving faith and undaunted resolution if any measure of success is to be achieved.

The process is one of orderly growth, having its sequential stages, like the growth of a tree; and as fruit can only be produced by carefully and patiently training the tree even so the pure and satisfying fruits of holiness can only be obtained by faithfully and patiently training the mind in the growth of right thought and conduct.

There are five steps in the overcoming of passion (which includes all bad habits and particular forms of wrong-doing) which I will call:

1. Repression   2. Endurance   3. Elimination

4. Understanding   5. Victory

When men fail to overcome their sins, it is because they try to begin at the wrong end. They want to have the stage of Victory without passing through the previous four stages. They are in the position of a gardener who wants to produce good fruit without training and attending to his trees.

Repression consists in checking and controlling the wrong act (such as an outburst of temper, a hasty or unkind word, a selfish indulgence etc.), and not allowing it to take actual form. This is equivalent to the gardener nipping off the useless buds and branches from his tree. It is a necessary process, but a painful one. The tree bleeds while undergoing the process, and the gardener knows that it must not be taxed too severely. The heart also bleeds when it refuses to return passion for passion, when it ceases to defend and justify itself. It is the process of "mortifying the members" of which St. Paul speaks.

But this repression is only the beginning of self-conquest. When it is made an end in itself, and there is no object of finally purifying the heart, that is a stage of hypocrisy; a hiding of one's true nature, and striving to appear better in the eyes of others than one really is. In that case it is an evil, but when adopted as the first stage toward complete purification, it is good. Its practice leads to the second stage of Endurance, or forbearance, in which one silently endures the pain which arises in the mind when it is brought in contact with certain actions and attitudes of other minds toward one. As success is attained in this stage, the striver comes to see that all his pain actually arises in his own weaknesses, and not in the wrong attitudes of others toward him, these latter being merely the means by which his sins are brought to the surface and revealed to him. He thus gradually exonerates all others from blame in his falls and lapses of conduct, and accuses only himself, and so learns to love those who thus unconsciously reveal to him his sins and shortcomings.

Having passed through these two stages of self-crucifixion, the disciple enters the third, that of Elimination, in which the wrong thought which lay behind the wrong act is cast from the mind immediately it appears. At this stage, conscious strength and holy joy begin to take the place of pain, and the mind having become comparatively calm, the striver is enabled to gain a deeper insight into the complexities of his mind, and thus to understand the inception, growth, and outworking of sin. This is the stage of Understanding.

Perfection in understanding leads to the final conquest of self, a conquest so complete that the sin can no more rise in the mind even as a thought or impression; for when the knowledge of sin is complete; when it is known in its totality, from its inception as a seed in the mind to its ripened outgrowth as act and consequence, then it can no more be allowed a place in life, but it is abandoned for ever. Then the mind is at peace. The wrong acts of others no longer arouse wrong and pain in the mind of the disciple. He is glad and calm and wise. He is filled with Love, and blessedness abides with him. And this is Victory!

CONTENTMENT IN ACTIVITY

The confounding of a positive spiritual virtue or principle with a negative animal vice is common amongst writers even of what is called the "Advance Thought School," and much valuable energy is frequently expended in criticising and condemning, where a little calm reasoning would have revealed a greater light, and led to the exercise of a broader charity.

The other day I came across a vigorous attack upon the teaching of "Love," wherein the writer condemned such teaching as weakly, foolish, and hypocritical. Needless to say, that which he was condemning as "Love," was merely weak sentimentality and hypocrisy.

Another writer in condemning "meekness" does not know that what he calls meekness is only cowardice, while another who attacks "chastity" as "a snare," is really confusing painful and hypocritical restraint with the virtue of chastity. And just lately I received a long letter from a correspondent who took great pains to show me that "contentment" is a vice, and is the source of innumerable evils.

That which my correspondent called "contentment" is, of course animal indifference. The spirit of indifference is incompatible with progress, whereas the spirit of contentment may, and does, attend the highest form of activity, the truest advancement and development. Indolence is the twin sister of indifference, but cheerful and ready action is the friend of contentment.

Contentment is a virtue which becomes lofty and spiritual in its later developments, as the mind is trained to perceive and the heart to receive the guidance, in all things, of a merciful law.

To be contented does not mean to forego effort; it means to free effort from anxiety; it does not mean to be satisfied with sin and ignorance and folly, but to rest happily in duty done, work accomplished.

A man may be said to be content to lead a grovelling life, to remain in sin and in debt, but such a man's true state is one of indifference to his duty, his obligations, and the just claims of his fellow-men. He cannot truly be said to possess the virtue of contentment; he does not experience the pure and abiding joy which is the accompaniment of active contentment; so far as his true nature is concerned he is a sleeping soul, and sooner or later will be awakened by intense suffering, having passed through which he will find that true contentment which is the outcome of honest effort and true living.

There are three things with which a man should be content:

1. With whatever happens.

2. With his friendships and possessions.

3. With his pure thoughts.

Contented with whatever happens, he will escape grief; with his friends and possessions, he will avoid anxiety and wretchedness; and with his pure thoughts, he will never go back to suffer and grovel in impurities.

There are three things with which a man should not be content:

1. With his opinions.

2. With his character.

3. With his spiritual condition.

Not content with his opinions, he will continually increase in intelligence; not content with his character, he will ceaselessly grow in strength and virtue; and not content with his spiritual condition, he will, everyday, enter into a larger wisdom and fuller blessedness. In a word, a man should be contented, but not indifferent to his development as a responsible and spiritual being.

The truly contented man works energetically and faithfully, and accepts all results with an untroubled spirit, trusting, at first, that all is well, but afterwards, with the growth of enlightenment, knowing that results exactly correspond with efforts. Whatsoever material possessions come to him, come not by greed and anxiety and strife, but by right thought, wise action, and pure exertion.

THE TEMPLE OF BROTHERHOOD

Universal Brotherhood is the supreme Ideal of Humanity, and towards that Ideal the world is slowly but surely moving.

Today, as never before, numbers of earnest men and women are striving to make this Ideal tangible and real; Fraternities are springing up on every hand, and Press and Pulpit, the world over, are preaching the Brotherhood of Man.

The unselfish elements in all such efforts cannot fail to have their effect upon the race, and are with certainty urging it towards the goal of its noblest aspirations; but the ideal state has not yet manifested through any outward organisation, and societies formed for the purpose of propagating Brotherhood are continually being shattered to pieces by internal dissension.

The Brotherhood for which Humanity sighs is withheld from actuality by Humanity itself; nay, more, it is frustrated even by men who work zealously for it is a desirable possibility; and this because the purely spiritual nature of Brotherhood is not perceived, and the principles involved, as well as the individual course of conduct necessary to perfect unity, are not comprehended.

Brotherhood as a human organisation cannot exist so long as any degree of self-seeking reigns in the hearts of men and women who band themselves together for any purpose, as such self-seeking must eventually rend the Seamless Coat of loving unity. But although organised Brotherhood has so far largely failed, any man may realise Brotherhood in its perfection, and know it in all its beauty and completion, if he will make himself of a wise, pure, and loving spirit, removing from his mind every element of strife, and learning to practice those divine qualities without which Brotherhood is but a mere theory, opinion, or illusive dream.

For Brotherhood is at first spiritual, and its outer manifestation in the world must follow as a natural sequence.

As a spiritual reality it must be discovered by each man for himself, and in the only place where spiritual realities can be found—within himself, and it rests with each whether he shall choose or refuse it.

There are four chief tendencies in the human mind which are destructive of Brotherhood, and which bar the way to its comprehension, namely:

- Pride
- Self-love
- Hatred
- Condemnation

Where these are there can be no Brotherhood; in whatsoever heart these hold sway, discord rules, and Brotherhood is not realised, for these tendencies are, in their very nature, dark and selfish and always make for disruption and destruction. From these four things proceeds that serpent brood of false actions and conditions which poison the heart of man, and fill the world with suffering and sorrow.

Out of the spirit of pride proceed envy, resentment, and opinionativeness. Pride envies the position, influence, or goodness of others; it thinks, "I am more deserving than this man or this woman"; it also continually finds occasion for resenting the actions of others, and says, "I have been snubbed," "I have been insulted," and thinking altogether of his own excellence, it sees no excellence in others.

From the spirit of self-love proceed egotism, lust for power, and disparagement and contempt. Self-love worships the personality in which it moves; it is lost in the adoration and glorification of that "I", that "self" which has no real existence, but is a dark dream and a delusion. It desires pre-eminence over others, and thinks, "I am great," "I am more important than others"; it also disparages others, and bestows upon them contempt, seeing no beauty in them, being lost in the contemplation of its own beauty.

From the spirit of hatred proceed slander, cruelty, reviling, and anger. It strives to overcome evil by adding evil to it. It says, "This man has spoken of me ill, I will speak still more ill of him and thus teach him a lesson." It mistakes cruelty for kindness, and causes its possessor to revile a reproving friend. It feeds the flames of anger with bitter and rebellious thoughts.

From the spirit of condemnation proceed accusation, false pity, and false judgement. It feeds itself on the contemplation of evil, and cannot see the good. It has eyes for evil only, and finds it in almost every thing and every person. It sets up an arbitrary standard of right and wrong by which to judge others, and it thinks, "This man does not do as I would have him do, he is therefore evil, and I will denounce him." So blind is the spirit of condemnation that whilst rendering its possessor incapable of judging himself, it causes him to set himself up as the judge of all the earth.

From the four tendencies enumerated, no element of brotherliness can proceed. They are deadly mental poisons, and he who allows them to rankle in his mind, cannot apprehend the peaceful principles on which Brotherhood rests.

Then there are chiefly four divine qualities which are productive of Brotherhood; which are, as it were, the foundation stones on which it rests, namely:

- Humility
- Self-surrender
- Love
- Compassion

Wheresoever these are, there Brotherhood is active. In whatsoever heart these qualities are dominant, there Brotherhood is an established reality, for they are, in their very nature, unselfish and are filled with the revealing Light of Truth. There is no darkness in them, and where they are, so powerful is their light, that the dark tendencies cannot remain, but are dissolved and dissipated.

Out of these four qualities proceed all those angelic actions and conditions which make for unity and bring gladness to the heart of man and to the world.

From the spirit of Humility proceed meekness and peacefulness; from self-surrender come patience, wisdom, and true judgment; from Love spring kindness, joy, and harmony; and from Compassion proceed gentleness and forgiveness.

He who has brought himself into harmony with these four qualities is divinely enlightened; he sees whence the actions of men proceed and wither they tend, and therefore can no longer live in the exercise of the dark tendencies. He has realised Brotherhood in its completion as freedom from malice; from envy, from bitterness, from contention, from condemnation. All men are his brothers, those who live in the dark tendencies, as well as those who live in the enlightened qualities, for he knows that when they have perceived the glory and beauty of the Light of Truth, the dark tendencies will be dispelled from their minds. He has but one attitude of mind towards all, that of good-will.

Of the four dark tendencies are born ill-will and strife; of the four divine qualities are born good-will and peace.

Living in the four tendencies a man is a strife-producer. Living in the four qualities a man is a peace-maker.

Involved in the darkness of the selfish tendencies, men believe that they can fight for peace, kill to make alive, slay injury by injuring, restore love by hatred, unity by contention, kindness by cruelty, and establish brotherhood by erecting their own opinions (which they themselves will, in the course of time, abandon as worthless) as objects of universal adoration.

The wished-for Temple of Brotherhood will be erected in the world when its four foundation stones of Humility, Self-surrender, Love, and Compassion are firmly laid in the hearts of men, for Brotherhood consists, first of all, in the abandonment of self by the individual, and its after-effects is unity between man and man.

Theories and schemes for propagating Brotherhood are many, but Brotherhood itself is one and unchangeable and consists in the complete cessation from egotism and strife, and in practising good-will and peace; for Brotherhood is a practice and not a theory. Self-surrender and Good-will are its guardian angels, and peace is its habitation.

Where two are determined to maintain an opposing opinion, the clinging to self and ill-will are there, and Brotherhood is absent.

Where two are prepared to sympathise with each other, to see no evil in each other, to serve and not to attack each other; the Love of Truth and Good-will are there, and Brotherhood is present.

All strifes, divisions, and wars inhere in the proud, unyielding self; all peace, unity, and concord inhere in the Principles which the yielding up of self reveals.

Brotherhood is only practiced and known by him whose heart is at peace with all the world.

PLEASANT PASTURES OF PEACE

He who aspires to the bettering of himself and humanity should ceaselessly strive to arrive at the exercise of that blessed attitude of mind by which he is enabled to put himself, mentally and sympathetically in the place of others, and so, instead of harshly and falsely judging them, and thereby making himself unhappy without adding to the happiness of those others, he will enter into their experience, will understand their particular frame of mind, and will feel for them and sympathise with them.

One of the great obstacles to the attainment of such an attitude of mind is, prejudice, and until this is removed it is impossible to act toward others as we would wish others to act toward us.

Prejudice is destructive of kindness, sympathy, love and true judgment, and the strength of a man's prejudice will be the measure of his harshness and unkindness toward others, for prejudice and cruelty are inseparable.

There is no rationality in prejudice, and, immediately it is aroused in a man he ceases to act as a reasonable being, and gives way to rashness, anger, and injurious excitement. He does not consider his words nor regard the feelings and liberties of those against whom his prejudices are directed. He has, for the time being, forfeited his manhood, and has descended to the level of an irrational creature.

While a man is determined to cling to his preconceived opinions, mistaking them for Truth, and refuses to consider dispassionately the position of others, he cannot escape hatred nor arrive at blessedness.

The man who strives after gentleness, who aspires to act unselfishly toward others, will put away all his passionate prejudice and petty opinions, and will gradually acquire the power of thinking and feeling for others, of understanding their particular state of ignorance or knowledge, and thereby entering fully into their hearts and lives, sympathising with them and seeing them as they are.

Such a man will not oppose himself to the prejudices of others by introducing his own, but will seek to allay prejudice by introducing sympathy and love, striving to bring out all that is good in men, encouraging the good by appealing to it, and discouraging the evil by ignoring it. He will realise the good in the unselfish efforts of others, though their outward methods may be very different from his own, and will so rid his heart of hatred, and will fit it with love and blessedness.

When a man is prone to harshly judge and condemn others, he should inquire how far he falls short himself; he should also reconsider those periods of suffering when he himself was misjudged and misunderstood, and, gathering wisdom and love from his own bitter experience, should studiously and self-sacrificingly refrain from piercing with anguish hearts that are as yet too weak to ignore, too immature and uninstructed to understand.

Sympathy is not required towards those who are purer and more enlightened than one's self, as the purer one lives above the necessity for it. In such a case reverence should be exercised, with a striving to lift one's self up to the purer level, and so enter into possession of the larger life. Nor can a man fully understand one who is wiser than himself, and before condemning, he should earnestly ask himself whether he is, after all, better than the man whom he has singled out as the object of his bitterness. If he is, let him bestow sympathy. If he is not, let him exercise reverence.

For thousands of years the sages have taught, both by precept and example, that evil is only overcome by good, yet still that lesson for the majority, remains unlearned. It is a lesson profound in its simplicity, and difficult to learn because men are blinded by the illusions of self. Men are still engaged in resenting, condemning, and fighting the evil in their own fellow-men, thereby increasing the delusion in their own hearts, and adding to the world's sum of misery and suffering. When they find out that their own resentment must be eradicated, and love put in its place, evil will perish for lack of sustenance.

"With burning brain and heart of hate,
I sought my wronger, early, late,
And all the wretched night and day
My dream and thought was slay, and slay.
My better self rose uppermost,
The beast within my bosom lost
Itself in love; peace from afar
Shone o'er me radiant like a star.
I Slew my wronger with a deed,
A deed of love; I made him bleed
With kindness, and I filled for years
His soul with tenderness and tears."

Dislike, resentment, and condemnation are all forms of hatred, and evil cannot cease until these are taken out of the heart.

But the obliterating of injuries from the mind is merely one of the beginnings in wisdom. There is a still higher and better way. And that way is so to purify the heart and enlighten the mind that, far from having to forget injuries, there will be none to remember. For it is only pride and self that can be injured and wounded by the actions and attitudes of others; and he who takes pride and self out of his heart can never think the thought, "I have been injured by another" or "I have been wronged by another."

From a purified heart proceeds the right comprehension of things; and from the right comprehension of things proceeds the life that is peaceful, freed from bitterness and suffering, calm and wise. He who thinks, "This man has injured me," has not perceived the Truth in life; falls short of that enlightenment which disperses the erroneous idea of evil as a thing to be hatefully resented. He who is troubled and disturbed about the sins of others is far from Truth; he who is troubled and disturbed about his own sins is very near to the Gate of Wisdom. He in whose heart the flames of resentment burn, cannot know Peace nor understand Truth; he who will banish resentment from his heart, will know and understand.

He who has taken evil out of his own heart cannot resent or resist it in others, for he is enlightened as to its origin and nature, and knows it as a manifestation of the mistakes of ignorance. With the increase of enlightenment, sin becomes impossible. He who sins, does not understand; he who understands does not sin.

The pure man maintains his tenderness of his heart toward those who ignorantly imagine they can do him harm. The wrong attitude of others toward him does not trouble him; his heart is at rest in Compassion and Love.

Blessed is he who has no wrongs to remember, no injuries to forget; in whose pure heart no hateful thought about another can take root and flourish.

Let those who aim at the right life, who believe that they love Truth, cease to passionately oppose themselves to others, and let them strive to calmly and wisely understand them, and in thus acting toward others they will be conquering themselves; and while sympathising with others, their own souls will be fed with the heavenly dews of kindness, and their hearts be strengthened and refreshed in the Pleasant Pastures of Peace.

Selections by James Allen

from

Byways of Blessedness

RIGHT BEGINNINGS

"All common things, each day's events,
That with the hour begin and end;
Our pleasures and our discontents
Are rounds by which we may ascend."

"We have not wings, we cannot soar;
But we have feet to scale and climb."
—Longfellow

"For common life, its wants
And ways, would I set forth in beauteous hues."
—Browning.

Life is full of beginnings. They are presented every day and every hour to every person. Most beginnings are small, and appear trivial and insignificant, but in reality they are the most important things in life.

See how in the material world everything proceeds from small beginnings. The mightiest river is at first a rivulet over which the grasshopper could leap; the great flood commences with a few drops of rain; the sturdy oak, which has endured the storms of a thousand winters, was once an acorn; and the smouldering match, carelessly dropped, may be the means of devastating a whole town by fire.

Consider, also, how in the spiritual world the greatest things proceed from smallest beginnings. A light fancy may be the inception of a wonderful invention or an immortal work of art; a spoken sentence may turn the tide of history; a pure thought entertained may lead to the exercise of a world-wide regenerative power; and a momentary animal impulse may lead to the darkest crime.

Have you yet discovered the vast importance of beginnings? Do you really know what is involved in a beginning? Do you know the number of beginnings you are continuously making, and realise their full import? If not, come with me for a short time, and thoughtfully explore this much ignored byway of blessedness, for blessed it is when wisely resorted to, and much strength and comfort it holds for the understanding mind.

A beginning is a cause, and as such it must be followed by an effect, or a train of effects, and the effect will always be of the same nature as the cause. The nature of an initial impulse will always determine the body of its results. A beginning also presupposes an ending, a consummation, achievement, or goal. A gate leads to a path, and the path leads to some particular destination; so a beginning leads to results, and results lead to a completion.

There are right beginnings and wrong beginnings, which are followed by effects of a like nature. You can, by careful thought, avoid wrong beginnings and make right beginnings, and so escape evil results and enjoy good results.

There are beginnings over which you have no control and authority—these are without, in the universe, in the world of nature around you, and in other people who have the same liberty as yourself.

Do not concern yourself with these beginnings, but direct your energies and attention to those beginnings over which you have complete control and authority, and which bring about the complicated web of results which compose your life. These beginnings are to be found in the realm of your own thoughts and actions; in your mental attitude under the variety of circumstances through which you pass; in your conduct day by day—in short, in your life as you make it, which is your world of good or ill.

In aiming at the life of Blessedness one of the simplest beginnings to be considered and rightly made is that which we all make everyday—namely, the beginning of each day's life.

How do you begin each day? At what hour do you rise? How do you commence your duties? In what frame of mind do you enter upon the sacred life of a new day? What answer can you give your heart to these important questions? You will find that much happiness or unhappiness follows upon the right or wrong beginning of the day, and that, when every day is wisely begun, happy and harmonious sequences will mark its course, and life in its totality will not fall far short of the ideal blessedness.

It is a right and strong beginning to the day to rise at an early hour. Even if your worldly duty does not demand it, it is wise to make of it a duty, and begin the day strongly by shaking off indolence. How are you to develop strength of will and mind and body if you begin every day by yielding to weakness? Self-indulgence is always followed by unhappiness. People who lie in bed till a late hour are never bright and cheerful and fresh, but are the prey of irritabilities, depressions, debilities, nervous disorders, abnormal fancies, and all unhappy moods. This is the heavy price which they have to pay for their daily indulgence. Yet, so blinding is the pandering to self that, like the drunkard who takes his daily dram in the belief that it is bracing up the nerves which it is all the time shattering, so the lie-a-bed is convinced that long hours of ease are necessary for him as a possible remedy for those very moods and weaknesses and disorders of which his indulgence is the cause. Men and women are totally unaware of the great losses which they entail by this common indulgence: loss of strength both of mind and body, loss of prosperity, loss of knowledge, and loss of happiness.

Begin the day, then, by rising early. If you have no object in doing so, never mind; get up, and go out for a gentle walk among the beauties of nature, and you will experience a buoyancy, a freshness, and a delight, not to say a peace of mind, which will amply reward you for your effort. One good effort is followed by another; and when a man begins the day by rising early, even though with no other purpose in view, he will find that the silent early hour is conducive to clearness of mind and calmness of thought, and that his early morning walk is enabling him to become a consecutive thinker, and so to see life and its problems, as well as himself and his affairs, in a clearer light; and so in time he will rise early with the express purpose of preparing and harmonising his mind to meet any and every difficulty with wisdom and calm strength.

There is, indeed, a spiritual influence in the early morning hour, a divine silence and an inexpressible repose, and he who, purposeful and strong, throws off the mantle of ease and climbs the hills to greet the morning sun will thereby climb no inconsiderable distance up the hills of blessedness and truth.

The right beginning of the day will be followed by cheerfulness at the morning meal, permeating the household with a sunny influence; and the tasks and duties of the day will be undertaken in a strong and confident spirit, and the whole day will be well lived.

Then there is a sense in which every day may be regarded as the beginning of a new life, in which one can think, act, and live newly, and in a wiser and better spirit.

> *"Every day is a fresh beginning;*
> *Every morn is the world made new,*
> *Ye who are weary of sorrow and sinning,*
> *Here is a beautiful hope for you,*
> *A hope for me and a hope for you."*

Do not dwell upon the sins and mistakes of yesterday so exclusively as to have no energy and mind left for living rightly today, and do not think that the sins of yesterday can prevent you from living purely today. Begin today aright, and, aided by the accumulated experiences of all your past days, live it better than any of your previous days; but you cannot possibly live it better unless you begin it better. The character of the whole day depends upon the way it is begun.

Another beginning which is of great importance is the beginning of any particular and responsible undertaking. How does a man begin the building of a house? He first secures a plan of the proposed edifice and then proceeds to build according to the plan, scrupulously following it in every detail, beginning with the foundation. Should he neglect the beginning—namely, the obtaining of a mathematical plan—his labour would be wasted, and his building, should it reach completion without tumbling to pieces, would be insecure and worthless. The same law holds good in any important work: the right beginning and first essential is a definite mental plan on which to build. Nature will have no slipshod work, no slovenliness, and she annihilates confusion, or rather, confusion is in itself annihilation. Order, definiteness, purpose eternally and universally prevail, and he who in his operations ignores these mathematical elements at once deprives himself of substantiality, completeness, success.

"Life without a plan,
As useless as the moment it began,
Serves merely as a soil for discontent
To thrive in, an encumbrance ere half spent."

Let a man start in business without having in his mind a perfectly formed plan to systematically pursue and he will be incoherent in his efforts and will fail in his business operations. The laws which must be observed in the building of a house also operate in the building up of a business. A definite plan is followed by coherent effort; and coherent effort is followed by well-knit and orderly results—to wit, completeness, perfection, success, happiness.

But not only mechanical and commercial enterprise—all undertakings, of whatsoever nature, come under this law. The author's book, the artist's picture, the orator's speech, the reformer's work, the inventor's machine, the general's campaign, are all carefully planned in the mind before the attempt to actualise them is commenced; and in accordance with the unity, solidarity, and perfection of the original mental plan will be the actual and ultimate success of the undertaking.

Successful men, influential men, good men are those who, amongst other things, have learned the value and utilised the power which lies hidden in those obscure beginnings which the foolish man passes by as "insignificant."

But the most important beginning of all—that upon which afflication or blessedness inevitably depends, yet is most neglected and least understood —is the inception of thought in the hidden, but causal region of the mind. Your whole life is a series of effects having their cause in thought—in your own thought. All conduct is made and moulded by thought; all deeds, good or bad, are thoughts made visible. A seed put into the ground is the beginning of a plant or tree; the seed germinates, the plant or tree comes forth into the light and evolves. A thought put into the mind is the beginning of a line of conduct: the thought first sends down its roots into the mind, and then pushes forth into the light in the forms of actions or conduct, which evolve into character and destiny.

Hateful, angry, envious, covetous, and impure thoughts are wrong beginnings, which lead to painful results. Loving, gentle, kind, unselfish and pure thoughts are right beginnings, which lead to blissful results. This is so simple, so plain, so absolutely true and yet how neglected, how evaded, and how little understood!

The gardener who most carefully studies how, when, and where to put in his seeds obtains the best results and gains the greater horticultural knowledge. The best crops gladden the soul of him who makes the best beginning. The man who most patiently studies how to put into his mind the seeds of strong, wholesome, and charitable thoughts, will obtain the best results in life, and will gain greater knowledge of truth. The greatest blessedness comes to him, who infuses into his mind the purest and noblest thoughts.

None but right acts can follow right thoughts; none but a right life can follow right acts—and by living a right life all blessedness is achieved.

He who considers the nature and import of his thoughts, who strives daily to eliminate bad thoughts and supplant them with good, comes at last to see that thoughts are the beginnings of results which affect every fibre of his being, which potently influence every event and circumstance of his life. And when he thus sees, he thinks only right thoughts, chooses to make only those mental beginnings which lead to peace and blessedness.

Wrong thoughts are painful in their inception, painful in their growth, and painful in their fruitage. Right thoughts are blissful in their inception, blissful in their growth, and blissful in their fruitage.

Many are the right beginnings which a man must discover and adopt on his way to wisdom; but that which is first and last, most important and all embracing, which is the source and fountain of all abiding happiness, is the right beginning of the mental operations—this implies the steady development of self-control, will-power, steadfastness, strength, purity, gentleness, insight, and comprehension. It leads to the perfecting of life, for he who thinks perfectly has abolished all unhappiness, his every moment is peaceful, his years are rounded with bliss—he has attained to the complete and perfect blessedness.

TRANSCENDING DIFFICULTIES AND PERPLEXITIES

"Man who man would be
Must rule the empire of himself; in it
Must be supreme, establishing his throne
On vanquished will, quelling the anarchy
Of hopes and fears, being himself alone."
—Shelley

"Have you missed in your aim? Well, the mark is still shining.
Did you faint in the race? Well, take breath for the next."
—Ellu Wheelar Wilcose.

To suggest that any degree of blessedness may be extracted from difficulties and perplexities will doubtless appear absurd to many; but truth is ever paradoxical, and the curses of the foolish are the blessings of the wise. Difficulties arise in ignorance and weakness, and they call for the attainment of knowledge and the acquisition of the strength.

As understanding is acquired by right living, difficulties become fewer, and perplexities gradually fade away, like the perishable mists which they are.

Your difficulty is not contained, primarily, in the situation which gave rise to it, but in the mental state with which you regard that situation and which you bring to bear upon it. That which is difficult to a child presents no difficulty to the matured mind of the man; and that which to the mind of an unintelligent man is surrounded with perplexity would afford no ground for perplexity to an intelligent man.

To the untutored and undeveloped mind of the child how great, and apparently insurmountable, appear the difficulties which are involved in the learning of some simple lesson. How many anxious and laborious hours and days, or even months, its solution costs; and, frequently, how many tears are shed in hopeless contemplation of the unmastered, and apparently insurmountable, wall of difficulty! Yet the difficulty is in the ignorance of the child only, and its conquest and solution is absolutely necessary for the development of intelligence and for the ultimate welfare, happiness, and usefulness of the child.

Even so is it with the difficulties of life with which older children are confronted, and which it is imperative, for their own growth and development, that they should solve and surmount; and each difficulty solved means so much more experience gained, so much more insight and wisdom acquired; it means a valuable lesson learned, with the added gladness and freedom of a task successfully accomplished.

What is the real nature of a difficulty? Is it not a situation which is not fully grasped and understood in all its bearings? As such, it calls for the development and exercise of a deeper insight and broader intelligence than has hitherto been exercised. It is an urgent necessity calling forth unused energy, and demanding the expression and employment of latent power and hidden resources. It is, therefore, a good angel, albeit disguised; a friend, a teacher; and, when calmly listened to and rightly understood, leads to larger blessedness and higher wisdom.

Without difficulties there could be no progress, no unfoldment, no evolution; universal stagnation would prevail, and humanity would perish of ennui.

Let a man rejoice when he is confronted with obstacles, for it means that he has reached the end of some particular line of indifference or folly, and is now called upon to summon up all his energy and intelligence in order to extricate himself, and to find a better way; that the powers within him are crying out for greater freedom, for enlarged exercise and scope.

No situation can be difficult of itself; it is the lack of insight into its intricacies, and the want of wisdom in dealing with it, which give rise to the difficulty. Immeasurable, therefore, is the gain of a difficulty transcended.

Difficulties do not spring into existence arbitrarily and accidentally; they have their causes, and are called forth by the law of evolution itself, by the growing necessities of the man's being. Herein resides their blessedness.

There are ways of conduct which end inevitably in complications and perplexities, and their are ways of conduct which lead, just as inevitably, out of troublesome complexities. Howsoever tightly a man may have bound himself round he can always unbind himself. Into whatsoever morasses of trouble and trackless wastes of perplexity he may have ignorantly wandered he can always find his way out again, can always recover the lost highway of uninvolved simplicity which leads, straight and clear, to the sunny city of wise and blessed action. But he will never do this by sitting down and weeping in despair, nor by complaining and worrying and aimlessly wishing he were differently situated. His dilemma calls for alertness, logical thought, and calm calculation. His position requires that he shall strongly command himself; that he shall think and search, and rouse himself to strenuous and unremitting exertion in order to regain himself.

Worry and anxiety only serve to heighten the gloom and exaggerate the magnitude of the difficulty. If he will but quietly take himself to task, and retrace, in thought, the more or less intricate way by which he has come to his present position, he will soon perceive where he made mistakes; will discover those places where he took a false turn, and where a little more thoughtfulness, judgement, economy, or self-denial would have saved him. He will see how, step by step, he has involved himself, and how a riper judgement and clearer wisdom would have enabled him to take an altogether different and truer course. Having proceeded thus far, and extracted from his past conduct this priceless grain of golden wisdom, his difficulty will already have assumed less impregnable proportions, and he will then be able to bring to bear upon it the searchlight of dispassionate thought, to thoroughly anatomise it, to comprehend it in all its details, and to perceive the relation which those details bear to the motive source of action and conduct within himself. This being done, the difficulty will have ceased, for the straight way out of it will plainly appear, and the man will thus have learned, for all time, his lesson; will have gained an item of wisdom and a measure of blessedness of which he can never again be deprived. Just as there are ways of ignorance, selfishness, folly, and blindness which end in confusion and perplexity, so there are ways of knowledge, self-denial, wisdom, and insight which lead to pleasant and peaceful consummations. He who knows this will meet difficulties in a courageous spirit, and, in overcoming them, will evolve truth out of error, bliss out of pain, and peace out of perturbation.

No man can be confronted with a difficulty which he has not the strength to meet and subdue. Worry is not merely useless, it is folly, for it defeats that power and intelligence which is otherwise equal to the task. Every difficulty can be overcome if rightly dealt with; anxiety is, therefore, unnecessary. The task which cannot be overcome ceases to be a difficulty, and becomes an impossibility; and anxiety is still unnecessary, for there is only one way of dealing with an impossibility—namely, to submit to it. The inevitable is the best.

> *"Heartily know,*
> *When half-gods go,*
> *The gods arrive."*

And just as domestic, social, and economic difficulties are born of ignorance and lead to riper knowledge, so every religious doubt, every mental-perplexity, every heart-beclouding shadow, presages greater spiritual gain, is prophetic of a brighter dawn of intelligence for him on whom it falls.

It is a great day in the life of a man (though at the time he knows it not) when bewildering perplexities concerning the mystery of life take possession of his mind, for it signifies that his era of dead indifference, of animal sloth, of mere vegetative happiness, has come to an end, and that henceforth he is to live as an aspiring, self-evolving being. No longer a mere human animal, he will now begin to live as a man, exerting all his mental energies to the solution of life's problems, to the answering of those haunting perplexities which are the sentinels of truth, and which stand at the gate and threshold of the Temple of Wisdom.

> *"He it is who, when great trials come,*
> *Nor seeks nor shuns them, but doth calmly stay."*

Nor will he ever rest again in selfish ease and listless ignorance; nor sleekly sate himself upon the swine's husks of fleshly pleasures; nor find a hiding-place from the ceaseless whisperings of his heart's dark and indefinable interrogatories. The divine within him has awakened; a sleeping god is shaking off the incoherent visions of the night, never again to slumber, never again to rest until his eyes rest upon the full, broad day of Truth.

It is impossible for such a man to hush, for any length of time, the call to higher purposes and achievements which is aroused within him, for the awakened faculties of his being will ceaselessly urge him on to the unravelling of his perplexities; for him there is no more peace in sin, no more rest in error, no final refuge but in Wisdom.

Great will be the blessedness of such a man when, conscious of the ignorance of which his doubts and perplexities are born, and acknowledging and understanding that ignorance, not striving to hide himself from it, he earnestly applies himself to its removal, seeks unremittingly, day after day, for that pathway of light which shall enable him to dispel all the dark shadows, dissolve his doubts, and find the solution to all his pressing problems. And as a child is glad when it has mastered a lesson long toiled over, just so a man's heart becomes light and free when he has satisfactorily met some worldly difficulty; even so, but to a far greater degree, is the heart of a man rendered joyous and peaceful when some vital and eternal question which has been long brooded over and grappled with is at last completely answered, and its darkness is for ever dispelled.

Do not regard your difficulties and perplexities as portentous of ill; by so doing you will make them ill; but regard them as prophetic of good, which, indeed, they are. Do not persuade yourself that you can evade them; you cannot. Do not try to run away from them; this is impossible, for wherever you go they will still be there with you—but meet them calmly and bravely; confront them with all the dispassion and dignity which you can command; weigh up their proportions; analyse them; grasp their details; measure their strength; understand them; attack them, and finally vanquish them. Thus will you develop strength and intelligence; thus will you enter one of those byways of blessedness which are hidden from the superficial gaze.

FORGIVENESS

"If men only understood
All the emptiness and acting
Of the sleeping and the waking
Of the souls they judge so blindly,
Of the hearts they pierce so unkindly,
They, with gentler words and feeling,
Would apply the balm of healing-
If they only understood."

"Kindness, nobler ever than revenge."
—Shakespeare.

The remembering of injuries is spiritual darkness; the fostering of resentment is spiritual suicide. To resort to the spirit and practice of forgiveness is the beginning of enlightenment; it is also the beginning of peace and happiness. There is no rest for him who broods over slights and injuries and wrongs; no quiet repose of mind for him who feels that he has been unjustly treated, and who schemes how best to act for the discomfiture of his enemy.

How can happiness dwell in a heart that is so disturbed by ill-will? Do birds resort to a burning bush wherein to build and sing? Neither can happiness inhabit in that breast that is aflame with burning thoughts of resentment. Nor can wisdom come and dwell where such folly resides.

Revenge seems sweet only to the mind that is unacquainted with the spirit of forgiveness; but when the sweetness of forgiveness is tasted then the extreme bitterness of revenge is known. Revenge seems to lead to happiness to those who are involved in the darkness of passion; but when the violence of passion is abandoned, and the mildness of forgiveness is restored to, then it is seen that revenge leads to suffering.

Revenge is a virus which eats into the very vitals of the mind, and poisons the entire spiritual being. Resentment is a mental fever which burns up the wholesome energies of the mind, and "taking offense" is a form of moral sickness which saps the healthy flow of kindliness and good-will, and from which men and women should seek to be delivered. The unforgiving and resentful spirit is a source of great suffering and sorrow, and he who harbours and encourages it, who does not overcome and abandon it, forfeits much blessedness, and does not obtain any measure of true enlightenment. To be hard-hearted is to suffer, is to be deprived of light and comfort; to be tender-hearted is to be serenely glad, is to receive light and be well comforted. It will seem strange to many to be told that the hard-hearted and unforgiving suffer most; yet it is profoundly true, for not only do they, by the law of attraction, draw to themselves the revengeful passions in other people, but their hardness of heart itself is a continual source of suffering. Every time a man hardens his heart against a fellow-being he inflicts upon himself five kinds of suffering—namely, the suffering of loss of love; the suffering of lost communion and fellowship; the suffering of a troubled and confused mind; the suffering of wounded passion or pride; and the suffering of punishment inflicted by others. Every act of unforgiveness entails upon the doer of that act these five sufferings; whereas every act of forgiveness brings to the doer five kinds of blessedness—the blessedness of love; the blessedness of increased communion and fellowship; the blessedness of a calm and peaceful mind; the blessedness of passion stilled and pride overcome; and the blessedness and kindness and good-will bestowed by others.

Numbers of people are today suffering the fiery torments of an unforgiving spirit, and only when they make an effort to overcome that spirit can they know what a cruel and exacting taskmaster they are serving. Only those who have abandoned the service of such a master for that of the nobler master of forgiveness can realise and know how grievous a service is the one, how sweet the other.

Let a man contemplate the strife of the world: how individuals and communities, neighbours and nations, live in continual retaliations towards each other; let him realise the heartaches, the bitter tears, the grievous partings and misunderstandings—yea, even the blood-shed and woe which spring from that strife—and, thus realising, he will never again yield to ignoble thoughts of resentment, never again take offense at the actions of others, never again live in unforgiveness towards any being.

> *"Have good-will*
> *To all that lives, letting unkindness die*
> *And greed and wrath; so that your lives be made*
> *Like soft airs passing by."*

When a man abandons retaliation for forgiveness he passes from darkness to light. So dark and ignorant is unforgiveness that no being who is at all wise or enlightened could descend to it; but its darkness is not understood and known until it is left behind, and the better and nobler course of conduct is sought and practiced. Man is blinded and deluded only by his own dark and sinful tendencies; and the giving up of all unforgiveness means the giving up of pride and certain forms of passion, the abandonment of the deeply-rooted idea of the importance of one-self and of the necessity for protecting and defending that self; and when that is done the higher life, greater wisdom, and pure enlightenment, which pride and passion completely obscured, are revealed in all their light and beauty.

Then there are petty offenses, little spites and passing slights, which, while of a less serious nature than deep-seated hatreds and revenges, dwarf the character and cramp the soul. They are due to the sin of self and self-importance and thrive on vanity. Whosoever is blinded and deluded by vanity will continually see something in the actions and the attitudes of others towards him at which to take offense, and the more there is of vanity the more greatly will the imaginary slight or wrong be exaggerated. Moreover, to live in the frequent indulgence of petty resentments increase the spirit of hatred, and leads gradually downward to greater darkness, suffering, and self-delusion. Don't take offense or allow your feelings to be hurt, which means—get rid of pride and vanity. Don't give occasion for offense or hurt the feelings of others, which means—be gently considerate, forgiving, and charitable towards all. The giving up—the total uprooting—of vanity and pride is a great task; but it is a blessed task, and it can be accomplished by constant practice in non-resentment and by meditating upon one's thoughts and actions so as to understand and purify them; and the spirit of forgiveness is perfected in one in the measure that pride and vanity are overcome and abandoned.

The not-taking-offense and the not-giving-offense go together. When a man ceases to resent the actions of others he is already acting kindly towards them, considering them before himself or his own defence. Such a man will be gently in what he says and does, will arouse love and kindness in others, and not stir them up to ill-will and strife. He will also be free from all fear concerning the actions of others towards him, for he who hurts none fears none. But the unforgiving man, he who is eager to "pay back" some real or imaginary slight or injury, will not be considerate towards others, for he considers himself first, and is continually making enemies; he also lives in the fear of others, thinking that that they are trying to do towards him as he is doing towards them. He who contrives the hurt of others fears others.

There is a beautiful story of Prince Dhirgayu which was told by an ancient Indian teacher to his disciples in order to impress them with the truth of the sublime percept that "hatred ceases not by hatred at any time; hatred ceases by not-hatred." The story is as follows:—Brahmadatta, a powerful king of Benares, made war upon Dirgheti, the king of Kosala, in order to annex his kingdom, which was much smaller than his own. Dirgheti, seeing that it was impossible for him to resist the greater power of bramhadatta, fled, and left his kingdom in his enemy's hands. For some time he wandered from place to place in disguise, and at last settled down with his queen in an artisan's cottage; and the queen gave birth to a son, whom they called Dirghayu.

Now, King Brahmadatta was anxious to discover the hiding-place of Dirgheti, in order to put to death the conquered king, for he thought, "Seeing that I have deprived him of his kingdom he may someday treacherously kill me If I do not kill him."

But many years passed away, and Dirgheti devoted himself to the education of his son, who by diligent application, became learned and skillful and wise.

And after a time Dirgheti's secret became known, and he, fearing that brahmadatta would discover him and slay all three, and thinking more of the life of his son than his own, sent away the prince. Soon after the exile king fell into the hands of Brahmadatta, and was, along with his queen, executed.

Now Brahmadatta thought: I have got rid of Dirgheti and his queen, but their son, Prince Dirghayu, lives, and he will be sure to contrive some means of effecting my assassination; yet he is unknown to any, and I have no means of discovering him." So the king lived in great fear and continual distress of mind.

Soon after the execution of his parents, Dirghayu, under an assumed name, sought employment in the king's stables, and was engaged by the master of elephants.

Dirghayu quickly endeared himself to all, and his superior abilities came at last under the notice of the king, who had the young man brought before him, and was so charmed with him that he employed him in his own castle, and he proved to be so able and diligent that the king shortly placed him in a position of great trust under himself.

One day the king went on a long hunting expedition, and became separated from his retinue, Dirghayu alone remaining with him. And the king, being fatigued with his exertions, lay down, and slept with his head in Dirghayu's lap.

Then Dirghayu thought: This king has greatly wronged me. He robbed my father of his kingdom, and slew my parents, and he is now entirely in my power." And he drew his sword, thinking to slay Brahmadatta. But, remembering how his father had taught him never to seek revenge but to forgive to the uttermost, he sheathed his sword.

At last the king awoke out of a disturbed sleep, and the youth inquired of him why he looked so frightened. "My sleep", said the king "is always restless, for I frequently dream that I am in the power of young Dirghayu and that he is alone to slay me. While lying here I again dreamed that with greater vividness than ever before and it has filled me with dread and terror.

Then the youth, drawing his sword, said: "I am Prince Dirghayu, and you are in my power, the time of vengeance has arrived."

Then the king fell upon his knees and begged Dirghayu to spare his life. And Dirghayu said: "It is you, O King! who must spare my life. For many years you have wished to find me in order that you might kill me; and, now that you have found me, let me beg of you to grant me my life."

And there and then did Brahmadatta and Dirghayu grant each other life, took hands, and solemnly vowed never to harm each other. And so overcome was the king by the noble and forgiving spirit of Dirghayu that he gave him his daughter in marriage, and restored to him his father's kingdom.

Thus hatred ceases by not-hatred—by forgiveness, which is very beautiful, and is sweeter and more effective than revenge. It is the beginning of love, of that divine love that does not seek its own; and he who practices it, who perfects himself in it, comes at last to realise that blessed state wherein the torments of pride and vanity and hatred and retaliation are forever dispelled, and good-will and peace are unchanging and unlimited. In that state of calm, silent bliss, even forgiveness passes away, and is no longer needed, for he who has reached it sees no evil to resent but only ignorance and delusion on which to have compassion, and forgiveness is only needed so long as there is any tendency to resent, retaliate, and take offense. Equal love towards all is the perfect law, the perfect state in which all lesser states find their completion. Forgiveness is one of the doorways in the faultless temple of Love Divine.

SEEING NO EVIL

"The solid, solid universe
Is pervious to love;
With bandaged eyes he never errs,
Around, below, above.
His blinding light
He flingeth white
On God's and Satan's brood,
And reconciles
By mystic wiles
The evil and the good."
—Emerson

If thou thinkest evil, be thou sure
Thine acts will bear the shadow of the stain;
And if thy thought be perfect, then thy deed
Will be as of the perfect, true, and pure.

After much practice in forgiveness and having cultivated the spirit of forgiveness up to a certain point, knowledge of the actual nature of good and evil dawns upon the mind, and a man begins to understand how thoughts and motives are formed in the human heart, how they develop, and how take birth in the form of actions. This marks the opening of a new vision in the mind, the commencement of a nobler, higher, diviner life; for the man now begins to perceive that there is no necessity to resist or resent the actions of others towards him, whatever those actions may be, and that all along his resentment has been caused by his own ignorance, and that his own bitterness of spirit is wrong. Having arrived thus far he will take himself with some such questionings as these: "Why this continual retaliation and forgiveness? Why this tormenting anger against another and then this repentance and forgiveness? Is not forgiveness the taking back of one's anger, the giving up of one's resentment; and if anger and resentment are good and necessary why repent of them and give them up? If it is so beautiful, so sweet, so peaceful to get rid of all feelings of bitterness and to utterly and wholly forgive, would it not be still more beautiful and sweet and peaceful never to grow bitter at all, never to know anger, never to resent as evil the action of another, but always to live in the experience of that pure, calm, blissful love which is known when an act of forgiveness is done, and all unruly passion towards another is put away? If another has done me wrong is not my hatred towards him wrong, and can one wrong right another? Moreover, has he by his wrong really injured me, or has he injured himself? Am I not injured by my own wrong rather than by his? Why, then, do I grow angry? Why do I resent, retaliate, and engage in bitter thoughts? Is it not because my pride is piqued or my vanity wounded or my selfishness thwarted? Is not because my blind animal passions are aroused and allowed to subdue my better nature? Seeing that I am hurt by another person's attitude towards me because of my own pride or vanity or ungoverned and unpurified passions, would it not be better to look to the wrong in myself rather than the wrong in another, to get rid of pride and vanity and passion, and so avoid being hurt at all?

By such self-questionings and their elucidation in the light of mild thoughts and dispassionate conduct a man, gradually overcoming passion and rising out of the ignorance which gave rise to passion, will at last reach that blessed state in which he will cease to see evil in others, and will dwell in universal good-will and love and peace. Not that he will cease to see ignorance and folly; not that he will cease to see suffering and sorrow and misery; not that he will cease to distinguish between acts that are pure and impure, right and wrong, for, having put away passion and prejudice, he will see these things in the full, clear light of knowledge, and exactly as they are; but he will cease to see anything—any evil power—in another which can do him injury, which he must violently oppose and strive to crush, and against which he must guard himself. Having arrived at right understanding of evil by purging it away from his own heart he sees that it is a thing that does not call for hatred and fear and resentment but for consideration, compassion, and love.

Shakespeare through one of his characters says: "There is no darkness but ignorance." All evil is ignorance, is dense darkness of mind, and the removal of sin from one's mind is a coming out of darkness into spiritual light. Evil is the negation of good, just as darkness is the negation, or absence of light, and what is there in a negation to arouse anger or resentment? When night settles down upon the world who is so foolish as to rail at the darkness? The enlightened man, likewise, does not accuse or condemn the spiritual darkness in men's hearts which is manifested in the form of sin, though by gentle reproof he may sometimes point out where the light lies.

Now the ignorance to which I refer as evil, or as the source of evil, is two-fold. There is wrong-doing which is committed without any knowledge of good and evil, and where there is no choice - this is unconscious wrong-doing. Then there is wrong-doing which is done in the knowledge that it ought not to be done—this is conscious wrong-doing; but both unconscious and conscious wrong-doing arise in ignorance—that is, ignorance of the real nature and painful consequences of the wrong-doing.

Why does a man continue to do certain things which he feels he ought not to do? If he knows that what he is doing is wrong where lies the ignorance?

He continues to do those things because his knowledge of them is incomplete. He only knows he ought not to do them by certain precepts without any qualms of conscience within, but he does not fully and completely understand what he is doing. He knows that certain acts bring him immediate pleasure, and so, in spite of the troubled conscience which follows that pleasure, he continues to commit them. He is convinced that the pleasure is good and desirable, and therefore to be enjoyed. He does not know that pleasure and pain are one, but thinks he can have the one without the other. He has no knowledge of the law which governs human actions, and never thinks of associating his sufferings with his own wrong-doing, but believes that they are caused by the wrong-doing of others or are the mysterious dispensations of Providence, and therefore not to be inquired into or understood. He is seeking happiness, and does those things which he believes will bring him most enjoyment, but he acts in entire ignorance of the hidden and inevitable consequences which attach to his actions.

Said a man to me once who was the victim of a bad habit: "I know the habit is a bad one, and that it does me more harm than good" I said: "If you know that what you are doing is bad and harmful why do you continue to do it?" And he replied: "Because it is pleasant, and I like it."

This man, of course, did not really know that his habit was bad. He had been told that it was, and he thought he knew or believed it was, but in reality he thought it was good, that it was conducive to his happiness and well-being, and therefore he continued to practice it. When a man knows by experience that a thing is bad, and that every time he does it he injures body or mind, or both; when his knowledge of that thing is so complete that he is acquainted with its hole train of baneful effects, then he cannot only not do it any longer, he cannot even desire to do it, and even the pleasure that was formerly in that thing becomes painful. No man would put a venomous snake in his pocket because it is prettily coloured. He knows that a deadly sting lurks in those beautiful markings. Nor, when a man knows the unavoidable pain and hurt which lie hidden in wrong thoughts and acts, does he continue to think and commit them. Even the immediate pleasure which formerly he greedily sought is gone from them; their surface attractiveness has vanished; he is no longer ignorant concerning their true nature; he sees them as they are.

I knew a young man who was in business, and although a member of a church, and occupying the position of voluntary religious instructor, he told me that it was absolutely necessary to practice lying and deception in business, otherwise sure and certain ruin would follow. He said he knew lying was wrong, but while he remained in business he must continue to do it. Upon questioning him I found, of course, that he had never tried truth and honesty in his business, had not even thought of trying the better way, so firmly convinced was he that it was not possible for him to know whether or not it would be productive or ruin. Now, did this young man know that lying was wrong? There was a preceptial sense only in which he knew, but there was a deeper and more real sense in which he did not know. He had been taught to regard lying as wrong, and his conscience bore out that teaching, but he believed that it brought to him profit, prosperity and happiness, and that honesty would bring him loss, poverty, and misery—in a word, he regarded lying, deep in his heart, as the right thing to do, and honesty as the wrong practice. He had no knowledge whatever of the real nature of the act of lying: how it is, on the instant of its committal, loss of character, loss of self-respect, loss of power, usefulness, and influence, and loss of blessedness; and how it unerringly leads to loss of reputation and loss of material profit and prosperity. Only when such a man begins to consider happiness of others, prefers to embrace the loss which he fears rather than clutch at the gain which he desires, will he obtain that real knowledge which lofty moral conduct alone can reveal; and then, experiencing the greater blessedness, he will see how, all along, he has been deceiving and defrauding himself rather than others, has been living in darkest ignorance and self-delusion.

These two common instances of wrong-doing will serve to illustrate and make plainer, to those of my readers who, while searching for Truth, are as yet doubtful, uncertain, and confused, the deep Truth that all sin, or evil, is a condition of ignorance and therefore to be dealt with in a loving and not a hateful spirit.

And as with bad habits and lying so with all sin—with lust, hatred, malice, envy, pride, vanity, self-indulgence and selfishness in all its forms; it is a state of spiritual darkness, the absence of the Light of Truth in the heart, the negation of knowledge.

Thus when, by overcoming the wrong condition in one's own heart, the nature of evil is fully realised and mere belief gives place to living knowledge, evil can no longer be hatefully condoned and violently resisted, and the wrong-doer is thought of with tender compassion.

And this brings us to another aspect of evil-namely, that of individual freedom; the right of every person to choose his own actions. Along with the seeing of evil in others is the desire to convert or coerce others into one's own ways of thinking and acting. Probably the commonest delusion in which men are involved is that of thinking that what they themselves believe and think and do is good, and all that is otherwise is evil, and therefore to be powerfully condemned and resisted. It is out of this delusion that all persecutions springs. There are Christians who regard all Atheists as men wholly evil, as given up to the service of an evil power; and there are Atheists who firmly believe that all christians are doing the greatest harm to the whole human race by their "superstitious and false doctrines." The truth is that neither the christian nor the Atheist is evil, nor in the service of evil, but each is choosing his own way, and is pursuing that course which he is convinced is right.

Let a man quietly contemplate the fact that numbers of followers of various religions the world over are, as they ever were, engaged in condemning each other as evil and wrong, and regarding themselves as good and right, and it will help him to realise how all evil is merely ignorance, spiritual darkness; and earnest meditation on that fact will be found to be one of the greatest aids in developing greater kindness, charity, insight and breadth of mind.

The truly wise and good man sees good in all, evil in none. He has abandoned the folly of wanting others to think and act as he thinks and acts, for he sees men are variously constituted, are at different points in their spiritual evolution, and must, of necessity, think and act differently. Having put away hatred, condemnation, egotism, and prejudice he has become enlightened, and sees that purity, love compassion, gentleness, patience, humility, and unselfishness are manifestations of light and knowledge; while impurity, hatred, cruelty, passion, darkness and ignorance; and that whether men are living in light or darkness they are one and all doing that which they think is necessary, are acting in accordance with their own measure of light or darkness. The wise man understands and understanding, he ceases from all bitterness and accusation.

Every man acts in accordance with his nature, with his own sense of right and wrong, and is surely gathering in the results of his own experience. There is one supreme right which every being possesses—to think and act as he chooses. If he chooses to think and act selfishly, thinking of his own immediate happiness only and not of that of others, then he will rapidly bring upon himself, by the action of the moral law of cause and effect, such afflictions as will cause him to pause and consider, and so find a better way. There is no teacher to compare with experience, no chastisement so corrective and purifying as that which men ignorantly inflict upon themselves. The selfish man is the ignorant man; he chooses his own way, but it is a way which leads to suffering, and through suffering to knowledge and bliss. The good man is the wise man; he likewise chooses his own way, but he chooses it in the full light of knowledge, having passed through the stages of ignorance and suffering, and arrived at knowledge and bliss.

A man begins to understand what "seeing no evil" is when, putting away all personal desires in his judgments of others, he considers them from their own standpoint, and judges their actions not from his own standard but from theirs. It is because men setup arbitrary standards of right and wrong, and are anxious that all should conform to their particular standard, that they see evil in each other. A man is only rightly judged when he is judged not from my standard or yours but from his own, and to deal with him thus is not judgment it is Love. It is only when we look through the eyes of Impersonal Love that we become enlightened, and see others as they really are; and a man is approaching that Love when he can say in his heart: "Who am I that I should judge another? Am I so pure and sinless that I arraign men and pass the judgment of evil upon them? Rather let me humble myself, and correct mine own errors, before assuming the position of supreme judge of those of other men."

It was said by one of old to those who were about to stone, as evil, a woman taken in the act of committing one of the darkest sins: "He that is without sin let him cast the first stone"; and though he who said it was without sin yet he took up no stone, nor passed any bitter judgment, but said, with infinite gentleness and compassion: "Neither do I condemn thee; go, and sin no more."

In the pure heart there is no room left where personal judgements and hatreds can find lodgement, for it is filled to overflowing with tenderness and love; it sees no evil; and only as men succeed in seeing no evil in others will they become free from sin and sorrow and suffering.

No man sees evil in himself or his own acts except the man who is becoming enlightened, and then he abandons those acts which he has come to see are wrong. Every man justifies himself in what he does, and, however evil others may regard his conduct, he himself thinks it to be good and necessary; If he did not he would not, could not do it. The angry man always justifies his anger; the covetous man his greed; the impure man his unchastity; the liar considers that his lying is altogether necessary; the slanderer believes that, in vilifying the characters of those whom he dislikes, and warning other people against their "evil" natures, he is doing well; the thief is convinced that stealing is the shortest and best way to plenty, prosperity, and happiness; and even the murderer thinks that there is a ground of justification for his deed.

Every man's deeds are in accordance with the measure of his own light or darkness, and no man can live higher than he is or act beyond the limits of his knowledge. Nevertheless, he can improve himself, and thereby gradually increase his light and extend the range of his knowledge. The angry man indulges in raillery and abuse because his knowledge does not extend to forbearance and patience. Not having practiced gentleness, he does not understand it, and cannot choose it; nor can he know, by its comparison with the light of gentleness, the darkness of anger. It is the same with the liar, the slanderer, and the thief; he lives in this dark condition of mind and action because he is limited to it by his immature knowledge and experience, because never having lived in the higher conditions, he has no knowledge of them, and it is, to him, as if they were non-existent: "The light shineth in the darkness and the darkness comprehendeth it not. Nor can he understand even the conditions in which he is living, because, being dark, they are necessarily devoid of all knowledge.

When a man driven by repeated sufferings to at last reflect upon his conduct, comes to see that his anger or lying, or whatever ignorant condition he may have been living in, is productive only of trouble and sorrow then he abandons it, and commences to search for , and practice, the opposite and enlightened condition; and when he is firmly established in the better way, so that his knowledge of both conditions is complete, then he realises in what great darkness he had formerly lived. This knowledge of good and evil by experience constitutes enlightment.

When a man begins to look, as it were, through the eyes of others, and to measure them by their own standard and not by his, then he ceases from seeing of evil in others, for he knows that every man's perception and standard of good and evil is different; that there is no vice so low but some men regard it as good; no virtue so high but some men regard it as evil; and what a man regards as good that to him is good; what he regards as evil that to him is evil.

Nor will the purified man, who has ceased to see evil in others, have any desire to win men to his own ways or opinions, but will rather help them in their own particular groove, knowing that an enlarged experience only, and not merely change of opinion can lead to higher knowledge and greater blessedness.

It will be found that men see evil in those who differ from them, good in those who agree with them. The man who greatly loves himself and is enamoured of his opinions will love all those who agree with him and will dislike all those who disagree with him. "If ye love them that love ye, what reward have ye? Love your enemies, do good to them that hate you." Egotism and vanity make men blind. Men of opposing religious views hate and persecute each other; men of opposing political views fight and condemn each other. The partisan measures all men by his own standard, and sets up his judgements accordingly. So convinced is he that he is right and others wrong that he at last persuades himself that to inflict cruelty on others is both good and necessary in order to coerce them into his way of thinking and acting, and so bring them to the right—his right—against their own reason and will.

Men hate, condemn, resist and inflict suffering upon each other, not because they are intrinsically evil, not because they are deliberately "wicked" and are doing, in the full light of truth, what they know to be wrong, but because they regard such conduct as necessary and right. All men are intrinsically good, but some are wiser than others, are older in experience than others. I recently heard, in substance, the following conversation between two men whom I will call D— and E—. The third person referred to as X is a prominent politician:—

E. Every man reaps the result of his own thoughts and deeds, and suffers for his own wrong.

D. If that is so, and if no man can escape from the penalty of his evil deeds, what an inferno some of our men in power must be preparing for themselves.

E. Whether a man is in power or not, so long as he lives in ignorance and sin, he will reap sorrow and suffering.

D. Look, for instance, at X—, a man totally evil, given up entirely to selfishness and ambition; surely great torments are reserved for so unprincipled a man.

E. But how do you know he is so evil.

D. By his works, his fruits. When I see a man doing evil I know that he is evil; and I cannot even think of X— but I burn with righteous indignation. I am sometimes inclined to doubt that there is an overruling power for good when I see such a man in a position where he can do so much harm to others.

E. What evil is he committing?

D. His whole policy is evil. He will ruin the country if he remains in power.

E. But while there are large numbers of people who think of X— as you do there are also large numbers, equally intelligent, who look on him as good and able, who admire him for his excellent qualities, and regard his policy as beneficent and making for national progress. He owes his position to these people; are they also evil?

D. They are deceived and mislead. And this only makes X's— evil all the greater, in that he can so successfully employ his talents in deceiving others in order to gain his own selfish ends. I hate the man.

E. May it not be possible that you are deceived?

D. In what way?

E. Hatred is self-deception; love is self-enlightenment. No man can see either himself or others clearly until he ceases from hatred and practices love.

D. That sounds very beautiful, but it is impracticable. When I see a man doing evil to others, and deceiving and misleading them, I must hate him. It is right that I should do so. X— is without a spark of conscience.

E. X— may or may not be all you believe to be, but, even if he is, according to your own words, he should be pitied and not condemned.

D. How so?

E. You say he is without a conscience.

D. Entirely so.

E. Then he is a mental cripple. Do you hate the blind because they cannot see, the dumb because they cannot speak, or the deaf because they cannot hear? When a captain has lost his rudder or broken his compass do you condemn him because he did not keep his ship off the rocks? Do you hold him responsible for the loss of life? If a man is totally devoid of conscience he is without the means of moral guidance, and all his selfishness must, perforce, appear to him good and right and proper. X— may appear evil to you, but is he evil to himself? Does he regard his own conduct as evil?

D. Whether he regards himself as evil or not he is evil.

E. If I were to regard you as evil because of your hatred for X— should I be right?

D. No.

E. Why not?

D. Because in such a case hatred is necessary, justifiable and righteous. There is such a thing as righteous anger, righteous hatred.

E. Is there such a thing as righteous selfishness, righteous ambition, righteous evil? I should be quite wrong in regarding you as evil, because you are doing what you are convinced is right, because you regard your hatred for X— as part of your duty as a man and a citizen; nevertheless, there is a better way than that of hatred, and it is the knowledge of this better way that prevents me from hating X— as you do, because however wrong his conduct might appear to me, it is not wrong to him nor to his supporters; moreover, all men reap as they sow.

D. What, then, is that better way?

E. It is the way of Love; the ceasing to regard others as evil. It is a blessed and peaceful state of heart.

D. Do you mean that there is a state which a man can reach wherein he will grow angry when he sees people doing evil?

E. No, I do not mean that, for while a man regards others as evil he will continue to grow angry with them; but I mean that a man can reach a state of calm insight and spotless love wherein he sees no evil to grow angry with, wherein he understands the various natures of men—how they are prompted to act, and how they reap, as the harvest of their own thoughts and deeds, the tares of sufferings and the corn of bliss. To reach that state is to regard all men with compassion and love.

D. The state that you picture is a very high one—it is, no doubt, a very holy and beautiful one—but it is a state that I should be sorry to reach; and

I should pray to be preserved from a state of mind were I could not hate a man like X— with an intense hatred.

Thus by this conversation it will be seen that D— regarded his hatred as good. Even so all men regard that which they do as necessary to be done. The things which men habitually practice those things they believe in. When faith in a thing wholly ceases it ceases to be practiced. D—'s individual liberty is equal to that of other men, and he has a right to hate another if he so wishes, nor will he abandon his hatred until he discovers, by the sorrow and unrest which it entails, how wrong and foolish and blind it is, and how, by its practice, he is injuring himself.

A great Teacher was once asked by one of His disciples to explain the distinction between good and evil, and holding His hand with the fingers pointing downward, He said: "Where is my hand pointing?"

And the disciple replied: "It is pointing downward."

Then, turning His hand upward, the Teacher asked: "Where now is my hand pointing?"

And the disciple answered: "It is pointing upward."

"That," said the Teacher, "is the distinction between evil and good."

By this simple illustration He indicated that evil is merely wrongly-directed energy, and good rightly-directed energy, and that the so-called evil man becomes good by reversing his conduct.

To understand the true nature of evil by living in the good is to cease to see other men as evil. Blessed is he who, turning from the evil in others exerts himself in the purification of his own heart. He shall one day become of "too pure eyes to behold evil."

Knowing the nature of evil, what does it behove a man to do? It behoves him to live only in that which is good: therefore if a man condemn me, I will not condemn him in return; if he revile me I will give him kindness; if he slander me I will speak of his good qualities, if he hate me then he greatly needs, and shall receive, my love. With the impatient I will be patient; with the greedy I will be generous, and with the violent and quarrelsome I will be mild and peaceable. Seeing no evil, whom should I hate or who regard as mine enemy?

"Were mankind murderous or jealous upon you, my brother, my sister? I'm so sorry for you. They are not murderous or jealous upon me; All has been gentle with me, I keep no account with lamentation; What have I to do with lamentation?"

He who sees men as evil imagines that behind those acts which are called "wicked" there is a corporate and substantial evil prompting those particular sins but he of stainless vision sees the deeds, themselves as the evil, and knows that there is no evil power, no evil soul or man behind those deeds. The substance of the universe is good; there is no substance of evil. Good alone is permanent; there is no fixed or permanent evil.

As brothers and sisters, born of the same parents and being of one household, love each other through all vicissitudes, see no evil in each other, but overlook all errors, and cling together in the strong bonds of affection— even so the good man sees humanity as one spiritual family, born of the same Father-Mother, being of the same essence and making for the same goal, and he regards all men and women as his brothers and sisters, makes no divisions and distinctions, sees none as evil, but is at peace with all. Happy is he who attains this blessed state.

ABIDING JOY

"Who carry music in their heart
Through dusky alone and wrangling mart,
plying their daily toil with busier feet,
Because their secret souls a holier repeat.

Serene will be our days and bright,
And happy will our nature be,
When love is an unerring light,
And joy its own security."
—Wordsworth

Abiding joy! Is there such a thing? Where is it? Who possesses it? Yea; there is such a thing. It is where there is no sin. It is possessed by the pure hearted.

As darkness is a passing shadow, and light is substance that remains, so sorrow is fleeting, but joy abides for ever. No true thing can pass away and become lost; no false thing can remain and be preserved. Sorrow is false, and it cannot live; joy is true, and it cannot die. Joy may become hidden for a time, but it can always be recovered; sorrow may remain for a period, but it can be transcended and dispersed.

Do not think your sorrow will remain; it will pass away like a cloud. Do not believe that the torments of sin are ever your portion; they will vanish like a hideous nightmare. Awake! arise! Be holy and Joyful!

You are the creator of your own shadows; you desire and then you grieve; renounce and then you rejoice.

You are not the impotent slave of sorrow; the Never-Ending Gladness awaits your Home-Coming. You are not the helpless prisoner of the darkness and dreams of sin; even now the beautiful light of holiness shines upon your sleeping lids, ready to greet your awakening vision.

In the heavy, troubled sleep of sin and self the abiding joy is lost and forgotten; its undying music is no more heard, and the fragrance of its fadeless flowers no longer cheers the heart of the wayfarer.

But when sin and self are abandoned, when the clinging to things for personal pleasure is put away, then the shadows of grief disappear, and the heart is restored to its Imperishable Joy.

Joy comes and fills the self-emptied heart; it abides with the peaceful; its reign is with the pure.

Joy flees from the selfish; it deserts the quarrelsome; it is hidden from the impure.

Joy is as an angel so beautiful and delicate and chaste that she can only dwell with holiness. She cannot remain with selfishness; she is wedded to Love. Every man is truly happy in so far as he is unselfish; he is miserable in so far as he is selfish. All truly good men, and by good men I mean those who have fought victoriously the battle against self, are men of joy. How great is the jubilation of the saint! No true teacher promises sorrow as the ultimate of life; he promises joy. He points to sorrow, but only as a process which sin has rendered necessary. Where self ends grief passes away. Joy is the companion of righteousness. In the divine life tender compassion fills the place where weeping sorrow sat. During the process of becoming unselfish there are periods of deep sorrow. Purification is necessarily severe. All becoming is painful. Abiding joy is its completion is realised only in the perfection of being, and this is

> *"A state*
> *Where all is loveliness, and power and love,*
> *With all sublimest qualities of mind,*
> *Where all*
> *Enjoy entire dominion o'er themselves.*
> *Acts, feelings, thoughts, conditions, qualities."*

Consider how a flower evolves and becomes; at first there is a little germ groping its way in the dark soil towards the upper light; then the plant appears, and leaf is added unto leaf; and finally the perfected flower appears, in the sweet perfume and chaste beauty of which all effort ceases.

So, with human life; at first the blind groping for the light in the dark soil of selfishness and ignorance; then the coming into the light, and the gradual overcoming of selfishness with its accompanying pain and sorrow; and finally the perfect flower of a pure, unselfish life, giving forth, without effort, the perfume of holiness and the beauty of joy.

The good, the pure, are the superlatively happy. However men may argumentatively deny or qualify this, humanity instinctively knows it to be true. Do not men everywhere picture their angels as the most joyful of beings? There are joyful angels in bodies of flesh; we meet them and pass on; and how many of those who come in contact with them are sufficiently pure to see vision within the form—to see the incorruptible angel in its common instrument of clay?

"They must grope who cannot see,
The blade before the ear must be;
The outward symbols disappear
From him whose inward sight is clear."

Yes; the pure are the joyful. We look almost in vain for any expressions of sorrow in the words of Jesus. The "Man of Sorrows" is only completed in the Man of Joy.

"I, Buddha, who wept with all my brother's tears,
Whose heart was broken by a whole world's woe,
Laugh and am glad, for there is Liberty!"

In sin, and in the struggle against sin, there is unrest and affliction, but in the perfection of Truth, in the path of Righteousness, there is abiding joy.

"Enter the Path! There spring the healing streams
Quenching all thirst! There bloomth immortal flowers
Carpeting all the way with joy! There throng
Swiftest and sweetest hours!"

Tribulation lasts only so long as there remains some chaff of self which needs to be removed. The tribulum, or threshing-machine, ceases to work when all the grain is separated from chaff; and when the last impurities are blown away from the soul, tribulation has completed its work, and there is no more need for it; then abiding joy is realised.

All the saints and prophets and saviours of the race have proclaimed with rejoicing the "Gospel" or the "Good News." All men know what Good News is—An impending calamity avoided, a disease cured, friends arrived or returned in safety, difficulties overcome, success in some enterprise assured —but what is the "Good News" of the saintly ones? This: that there is peace for the troubled, healing for the afflicted, gladness for the grief-stricken, victory for the sinful, a homecoming for the wanderer, and joy for the sorrowing and broken-hearted. Not that these beautiful realities shall be in some future world, but they are here and now, that they are known and realised and enjoyed; and are, therefore, proclaimed that all may accept them who will break the galling bonds of self and rise into the glorious liberty of unselfish love.

Seek the highest Good, and as you find it, as you practice it and realise it, you will taste the deepest, sweetest joy. As you succeed in forgetting your own selfish desires in your thoughtfulness for others, in your care for others, in your service for others, just so far and no further will you find and realise the abiding joy in life.

Inside the gateway of unselfishness lies the elysium of Abiding Joy, and whosoever will may enter in, whosoever doubts let him come and see.

And knowing this—that selfishness leads to misery, unselfishness to joy, not merely for one's self alone—for if this were all how unworthy could be our endeavours! But for the whole world and because all with whom we live and come in contact will be the happier and truer for our unselfishness; because Humanity is one, and the joy of one is the joy of all—knowing this let us scatter flowers and not thorns in the common ways of life—yea, even in the highway of our enemies let us scatter the blossoms of unselfish love —so shall the pressure in their footprints fill the air with the perfume of holiness and gladden the world with the aroma of joy.

SILENTNESS

"Be still! The crown of life is silentness.
Give thou a quiet hour to each long day,
Too much of time we spend in profitless
And foolish talk. Too little do we say.

If thou wouldst gather words that shall avail,
Learning a wisdom worthy to express,
Leave for a while thy chat and empty tale—
Study the golden speech of silentness."
—A.L.Salmon.

"Be still, my soul.
Rest awhile from the feverish activities in
which you lose yourself.
Be not afraid to be left alone with yourself
for one short hour."
—Ernest Crosly.

In the words of a wise man there is great power, but his silence is more powerful still. The greatest men teach us most effectively when they are purposely silent. The silent attitude of the great man noted, perhaps, by one or two of his disciples only is recorded and preserved through the ages; while the obtrusive words of the merely clever talker, heard, perhaps, by thousands, and at once popularised, are neglected and forgotten in, at most, a few generations. The silence of Jesus, when asked by Pilate "What is Truth?" is the impressive, the awful silence of profound wisdom; it is pregnant with humility and reproof, and perpetually rebukes that shallowness that, illustrating the truth that "fools step in where angels fear to tread," would in terms of triteness parcel out the universe, or think to utter the be-all and the end-all of the mystery of things in some textual formula or theological platitude. When, plied with questions about Brahma (God) by the argumentative Brahmans, Buddha remained silent, he taught them better than they knew, and if by his silence he failed to satisfy the foolish he thereby profoundly instructed the wise. Why all this ceaseless talk about God, with its accompaniment of intolerance? Let men practice some measure of kindliness and good-will, and thereby acquaint themselves with the simple rudiments of wisdom. Why all these speculative arguments about the nature of God? Let us first understand somewhat of ourselves. There are no greater marks of folly and moral immaturity than irreverence and presumption; no greater manifestations of wisdom and moral maturity than reverence and humility. Lao-Tze, in his own life, exemplified his teaching that the wise man "teaches without words." Disciples were attracted to him by the power which ever accompanies a wise reserve. Living in comparative obscurity and silence, not courting the ear of men, and never going out to teach, men sought him out and learned of him wisdom.

The silent acts of the Great Ones are beacons to the wise, illuminating their pathway with no uncertain radiance, for he would attain to virtue and wisdom must learn, not only when to speak and what to say, but also when to remain silent and what not to say. The right control of the tongue is the beginning of wisdom; the right control of the mind is the consummation of wisdom. By curbing his tongue a man gains possession of his mind, and to have complete possession of one's mind is to be a Master of Silence.

The fool babbles, gossips, argues, and bandies words. He glories in the fact that he has had the last word and has silenced his opponent. He exults in his own folly, is ever on the defensive, and wastes his energies in unprofitable channels. He is like a gardener who continues to dig and plant in unproductive soil.

The wise man avoids idle words, gossip, vain argument, and self-defence. He is content to appear defeated; rejoices when he is defeated, knowing that, having found and removed another error in himself he has thereby become wiser. Blessed is he who does not strive for the last word!

"Backward I see in my own days where I sweated through
fog with linguists and contenders;
I have no mockings or arguments, I witness and wait"

Silence under provocation is the mark of a cultured and sympathetic soul. The thoughtless and unkind are stirred by every slight provocation, and will lose their mental balance by even the appearance of a personal encroachment. The self-possession of Jesus is not a miracle; it is the flower of culture, the diadem of wisdom. When we read of Jesus that "He answered never a word" and of Buddha that "He remained silent," we get a glimpse of the vast power of silence, of the silent majesty of true greatness.

The silent man is the powerful man. The victim of garrulity is devoid of influence; his spiritual energies are dissipated. Every mechanic knows that before a force can be utilised and definitely directed it must be conserved and stored; and the wise man is a spiritual mechanic who conserves the energies of his mind, holds them in masterful abeyance, ready at any moment to direct them, with effective purpose, to the accomplishment of some necessary work.

The true strength is in silentness. It is well said that "The dog that barks does not bite." The grim and rarely broken silence of the bull-dog is the necessary adjunct to that powerfully concentrated and effectual action for which the animal is known and feared. This, of course, is a lower form of silentness, but the principle is the same. The boaster fails; his mind is diverted from the main purpose; and his energies are frittered away upon self-glorification. His forces are divided between his task and the reward to himself, the greater portion going to feed the lust of reward. He is like an unskilful general who loses the battle through dividing his forces instead of concentrating them upon a point. Or he is like a careless engineer who leaves open the waste-valve of his engine and allows the steam to run down. The modest, silent, earnest man succeeds: freed from vanity, and avoiding the dissipation of self-glorification, all his powers are concentrated upon the successful performance of his task. Even while the other man is talking about his powers he is already about his work, and is so much nearer than the other to its completion. It is a law everywhere and always that energy distributed is subject unto energy conserved. The noisy and boasting Charles will ever be thrown by the quiet and modest Orlando.

It is a law universally applicable that quietness is strength. The business man who succeeds never talks about his plans, methods, and affairs, and should he, turned giddy by success, begin to do this he will then commence to fail. The man of great moral influence never talks about himself and his spiritual victories, for should he do so, in that moment his moral power and influence would be gone, and, like Samson, he would be shorn of his strength. Success, worldly or spiritual, is the willing servant of strong, steady, silent, unflinching purpose. The most powerful disintegrating forces make no noise. The greatly-overcoming mind works silently.

If you would be strong, useful, and self-reliant learn the value and power of silentness. Do not talk about yourself. The world instinctively knows that the vain talker is weak and empty, and so it leaves him to his own vanity. Do not talk about what you are going to do but do it, and let your finished work speak for itself. Do not waste your forces in criticising and disparaging the work of others but set about to do your own work thoroughly and well. The worst work with earnestness and sweetness behind it is altogether better than barking at others. While you are disparaging the work of others you are neglecting your own. If others are doing badly help and instruct them by doing better yourself. Neither abuse others nor account their abuse of any weight. When attacked remain silent: in this way you will conquer yourself, and will, without the use of words, teach others.

But the true silence is not merely a silent tongue; it is a silent mind. To merely hold one's tongue, and yet to carry about a disturbed and rankling mind, is no remedy for weakness and no source of power. Silentness, to be powerful, must envelop the whole mind, must permeate every chamber of the heart; it must be the silence of peace. To this broad, deep, abiding silentness a man attains only in the measure that he conquers himself. While passions, temptations, and sorrows disturb, the holier, profounder depths of silence are yet to be sounded. To smart under the words and actions of others means that you are yet weak, uncontrolled, unpurified. So rid your heart of the disturbing influences of vanity and pride and selfishness that no petty spite can reach you, no slander or abuse disturb your serene repose. As the storm rages ineffectually against a well-built house, while its occupant sits composed and happy by his fire side within, so no evil without can disturb or harm him who is well fortified with wisdom; self-governed and silent, he remains at peace within. To this great silence the self-conquered man attains.

> *"Envy and calumny, and hate and pain,*
> *And that unrest which men miscall delight,*
> *Can touch him not, nor torture him again"*

There is no commoner error amongst men than that of supposing that nothing can be accomplished without much talking and much noise. The busy, shallow talker regards the quiet thinker or silent doer as a man wasted; he thinks silentness means "doing nothing", and that hurrying, bustling, and ceaseless talking means "doing much." He also confounds popularity with power. But the thinker and doer is the real and effectual worker. His work is at the root and core and substance of things, and as Nature silently, yet with hidden and wondrous alchemy, transmutes the rude elements of earth and air into tender leaves, beautiful flowers, delectable fruits,—yea into a myriad forms of beauty—even so does the silent purposeful worker transform the ways of men and the face of the world by the might and magic of his silently-directed energy. He wastes no time and force in tinkering with the ever-changing and artificial surface of things, but goes to the living vital centre, and works therefrom and thereon; and in due season, perhaps when his perishable form is withdrawn from the world, the fruits of his obscure but imperishable labours come forth to gladden the world. But the words of the talker perish. The world reaps no harvest from the sowing of sound.

He who conserves his mental forces also conserves his physical forces. The strongly quiet, calm man lives to a greater age, and in the possession of better health than the hurrying, noisy man. Quiet, subdued mental harmony is conducive to physical harmony—health. The followers of George Fox are today the healthiest, longest-lived and most successful portion of the British community, and they live quiet, unostentatious, purposeful lives, avoiding all worldly excitements and unnecessary words. They are a silent people, all their meetings being conducted on the principle that "Silence is Power."

Silentness is powerful because it is the outcome of self-conquest, and the more successfully a man governs himself the more silent he becomes. As he succeeds in living to a purpose and not to the pleasures of self he withdraws himself from the outer discords of the world and reaches to the inward music of peace. Then when he speaks there is purpose and power behind his words, and when he maintains silence there is equal or even greater power therein. He does not utter that which is followed by pain and tears; does not do that which is productive of sorrow and remorse. But, saying and doing those things only which are ripe with thoughtfulness, his conscience is quiet, and all his days are blessed.

STANDING ALONE

"By all means use to be alone,
Salute thyself; see what thy soul doth wear."
—George Herbert.
He that has light within his own clear breast
My sit in the centre and enjoy bright day."
—Milton.

In the life of blessedness self-reliance is of the utmost importance. If there is no peace there must be strength; if there is to be security there must be stability; if there is to be lasting joy there must be no leaning upon things which at any moment may be snatched away for ever.

A man does not commence to truly live until he finds an immovable centre within himself on which to stand, by which to regulate his life, and from which to draw his peace. If he trusts to that which fluctuates he also will fluctuate; if he leans upon that which may be withdrawn he will fall and be bruised; if he looks for satisfaction in perishable accumulations he will starve for happiness in the midst of plenty.

Let a man learn to stand alone, looking to no one for support; expecting no favours, craving no personal advantages; not begging, nor complaining, not craving, nor regretting, but relying upon the truth within himself, deriving his satisfaction and comfort from the integrity of his own heart.

If a man can find no peace within himself where shall he find it? If he dreads to be alone with himself what steadfastness shall he find in company? If he can find no joy in communion with his own thoughts how shall he escape misery in his contact with others? The man who has yet found nothing within himself upon which to stand will nowhere find a place of constant rest.

Men everywhere are deluded by the superstition that their happiness rests with other people and with outward things, and, as a result, they live in continual disappointments, regrets, and lamentations. The man who does not look for happiness to any others or to external things, but finds within himself its inexhaustible source, will be self-contained and serene under all circumstances, and will never become the helpless victim of misery and grief. The man who looks to others for support, who measures his happiness by the conduct of others and not by his own, who depends upon their co-operation for his peace of mind—such a man has no spiritual foothold, his mind is tossed hither and thither with the continual changes going on around him, and he lives in that ceaseless ebb and flow of the spirits which is wretchedness and unrest. He is a spiritual cripple, and has yet to learn how to maintain his mental centre of gravity, and so go without the aid of crutches.

As a child learns to walk in order to go about from place to place of itself strong and unaided, so should a man learn to stand alone, to judge and think and act for himself, and to choose, in the strength of his own mind, the oathway which he shall walk.

Without is change and decay and insecurity, within is all surety and blessedness. The soul is sufficient of itself. Where the need is there is the abundant supply. Your eternal dwelling-place is within; go there and take possession of your mansion; there you are a king, elsewhere you are a vassal. Be contended that others shall manage or mismanage their own little kingdom, and see to it that you reign strongly over your own. Your entire well-being and the well-being of the whole world lies there. You have a conscience, follow it; you have a mind, clarify it; you have a judgment, use and improve it; you have a will, employ and strengthen it; you have knowledge, increase it; there is a light within your soul, watch it, tend it, encourage it, shield it from the winds of passion, and help it to burn with a steadier and ever steadier radiance. Leave the world and come back to yourself. Think as a man, act as a man, live as a man. Be rich in yourself, be complete in yourself. Find the abiding centre within you and obey it. The earth is maintaining its orbit by its obedience to its centre the sun. Obey the centre of light that is within you; let others call it darkness if they will. You are responsible for yourself, are accountable to yourself, therefore rely upon yourself. If you fear yourself who will place confidence in you? If you are untrue to yourself where shall you find the sweet satisfaction of Truth?

The great man stands alone in the simple dignity of independent manhood; he pursues his own path fearlessly, and does not apologise or "beg leave." Criticism and applause are no more to him than the dust upon his coat, of which he shakes himself free. He is not guided by the changing opinions of men but guides himself by the light of his own mind. Other men barter away their manhood for messes of flattery or fashion.

Until you can stand alone, looking for guidance neither to spirits nor mortals, gods nor men, but guiding yourself by the light of the truth within you, you are not unfettered and free, not altogether blessed. But do not mistake pride for self-reliance. To attempt to stand upon the crumbling foundation of pride is to be already fallen. No man depends upon others more than the proud man. He drinks in their approbation and resents their censure. He mistakes flattery for sound judgment, and is most easily hurt or pleased by the opinions of others. His happiness is entirely in the hands of others. But the self-reliant man stands, not upon personal pride, but on an abiding law, principle, ideal, reality within himself. Upon this he poises himself, refusing to be swept from his strong foothold either by the waves of passion within or the storms of opinion without, but should he at any time lose his balance he quickly regains himself, and is fully restored. His happiness is entirely in his own hands.

Find your centre of balance and succeed in standing alone, and, whatever your work in life may be, you will succeed; you will accomplish what you set your mind upon , for the truly self-reliant man is the invincible man. But though you do not rely upon others, learn of them. Never cease to increase in knowledge, and be ever ready to receive that which is good and useful. You can not have too much humility; the most self-reliant men are the most humble. "No aristocrat, no prince born to the purple, can begin to compare with the self-respect of the saint. Why is he lowly, but that he knows that he can well afford it, resting on the largeness of God in him." Learn of all men, and especially of the masters of Truth, but do not lose your hold upon the truth that the ultimate guidance is in yourself. A master can say: "Here is the path," but he can neither compel you to walk it, nor walk it for you. You must put forth your own efforts , must achieve by your own strength, must make his truth your truth by your own unaided exertions; you must implicitly trust yourself.

> "This thing is God—to be Man with thy might,
> To grow great in the strength of thy spirit,
> And live out thy life as the light."

You are to be master of yourself, lord over yourself, not fawning and imitating, but doing your work as a living, vital portion of the universe; giving love but not expecting it; giving sympathy but not craving for it; giving aid but not depending upon it. If men should censure your work, heed them not. It sufficeth that your work be true: rest you in this sufficiency. Do not ask: "Will my work please?" but: "Is it real?" If your work be true the criticism of men cannot touch it; if it be false their disapproval will not slay it quicker than it will die of itself. The words and acts of Truth cannot pass away until their work is fully accomplished; the words and acts of error cannot remain, for they have no work to do. Criticism and resentment are alike superfluous.

Free yourself from the self-imposed tyranny of slavish dependence, and stand alone, not as an isolated unit, but as a sympathetic portion of the whole. Find the Joy that results from well—earned freedom, the peace that flows from wise self-possession, the blessedness that inheres in native strength.

> *"Honour to him who, self-complete, if lone,*
> *Carves to the grave one pathway all his own,*
> *And heeding naught that men may think or say,*
> *Asks but his soul if doubtful of the way."*

UNDERSTANDING THE SIMPLE LAWS OF LIFE

"Watch narrowly
The demonstration of a truth, its birth,
And you trace back the effluence to its spring
And source within us."
—*Browning.*

"More is the treasure of law than gems;
Sweeter than comb its sweetness. Its delights,
Delightful past compare."
—*The Light of Asia.*

Walking those byways which I have so far pointed out, resting in their beauty and drinking in their blessedness, the pilgrim along life's broad highway will in due time come to one wherein his last burden will fall from him, where all his weariness will pass away, where he will drink of light-hearted liberty, and rest in perpetual peace. And this most blessed of spiritual byways, the richest source of strength and comfort, I call The Right Understanding of the Simple Laws of Life. He who comes to it leaves behind him all lack and longing, all doubt and perplexity, all sorrow and uncertainty. He lives in the fullness of satisfaction, in light and knowledge, in gladness and surety. He who comprehends the utter simplicity of life, who obeys its laws and does not step aside into the dark paths and complex mazes of selfish desire, stands where no harm can reach him, where no enemy can lay him low—and he doubts, desires, and sorrows no more. Doubt ends where reality begins; painful desire ceases where the fullness of joy is perpetual and complete; and when the Unfailing and Eternal Good is realised what room is there for sorrow?

Human life when rightly lived is simple with a beautiful simplicity, but it is not rightly lived while it is bound to a complexity of lusts, desires, and wants—these are not the real life but the burning fever and painful disease which originate in an unenlightened condition of mind. The curtailing of one's desires is the beginning of wisdom; their entire mastery its consummation. This is so because life is bounded by law, and ,being inseparable from law, life has no need that is not already supplied. Now lust, or desire, is not need, but a rebellious superfluity, and as such it leads to deprivation and misery. The prodigal son, while in his father's house, not only had all that he required, but was surrounded by a superabundance. Desire was not necessary, because all things were at hand; but when desire entered his heart he "went into a far country," and "began to be in want," and it was only when he became reduced to the utmost extremity of starvation that he turned with longing towards his father's home. This parable is symbolic of the evolution of the individual and the race. Man has come into such a complexity of carvings that he lives in continual discontent, dissatisfaction, want, and pain; and his only cure lies in a return to the Father's Home—that is, to actual living or being as distinguished from desiring. But a man does not do this until he is reduced to the last extremity of spiritual starvation ; he has then reaped the experience of pain and sorrow as the result of desire, and looks back with longing towards the true life of peace and plenty; and so he turns round, and begins his toilsome journey back towards his Home, towards that rich life of simple being wherein is emancipation from the thraldom and fever and hunger of desire, and this longing for the true life, for Truth, Reality, should not be confounded with desire: it is aspiration. Desire is the craving for possession:aspiration is the hunger of the heart for peace. The craving for things leads ever farther and farther from peace, and not only ends in deprivation but is, in itself, a state of perpetual want. Until it comes to an end rest, satisfaction, is an impossibility. The hunger for things can never be satisfied, but the hunger for peace can and the satisfaction of peace is found, is fully possessed, when all selfish desire is abandoned. Then there is fullness of joy, abounding plenty, and rich and complete blessedness. In this supremely blessed state life is comprehended in its perfect symmetry and simplicity and the acme of power and usefulness is attained. Then even the hunger for peace ceases, for peace becomes the normal condition, is fully possessed, constant and never-varying. Men, immersed in desire, ignorantly imagine that the conquest of desire, leads to inactivity, loss of power, and lifelessness. Instead, it leads to highly concentrated activity, to the full employment of power, and to a life so rich, so glorious, and so abundantly blessed as to be incomprehensible to those who hunger for pleasures and possessions. Of this life only can it be said:

"Here are no sounds of discord—no profane
Or senseless gossip of unworthy things-
Only the songs of chisels and of pens,
Of busy brushes, and ecstatic strains
Of souls surcharged with music most divine
Here is no idle sorrow, no poor grief
For any day or object left behind

121

For time is counted precious, and herein
Is such complete abandonment of Self
That tears turn into rainbows, and enhance
The beauty of the land where all is fair."

When a man is rescued from selfish desire his mind is unencumbered, and he is free to work for humanity. No longer racing after those gratifications which leave him hungry still, all his powers are at his immediate command. Seeking no rewards he can concentrate all his energies upon the faultless completion of his duties, and so accomplish all things and fulfil all righteousness.

The fully enlightened and fully blessed man is not prompted to action by desire but works from knowledge. The man of desire needs the promise of reward to urge him to action. He is as a child working for the possession of a toy. But the man of knowledge, living in the fullness of life and power, can at any moment bring his energies into requisition for the accomplishment of that which is necessary. He is, spiritually, a full-grown man; for him all rewards have ceased; to him all occurrences are good; he lives always in complete satisfaction. Such a man has attained to life, and his delight (and it is a sweet, perpetual, and never-failing delight) is in obedience to the simple demands of exact and never-failing law.

But this life of supreme blessedness is an end, and the pilgrim who is striving towards it, the prodigal returning to it, must travel thither, and employ means to get there. He must pass through the country of his animal desires, disentangling himself from their intricacies, simplifying them, overcoming them; this is the way, and he has no enemies but what spring within himself. At first the way seems hard because, blinded by desire, he does not perceive the simple structure of life, and its laws are hidden from him; but as he becomes more simple in his mind the direct laws of life become unfolded to his spiritual perception, and at once the point is reached where these laws begin to be understood and obeyed; then the way becomes plain and easy; there is no more uncertainty and darkness, but all is seen in the clear light of knowledge.

It will help to accelerate the progress of the searcher for the true and blessed life if we now turn to a consideration of some of these simple laws which are rigidly mathematical in their operations.

"The elementary laws never apologise."

All life is one, though it has a diversity of manifestations; all law is one, but it is applicable and operative in a variety of ways. There is not one law for matter and another for mind, not one for the material and visible and another for the spiritual and invisible; there is the same law throughout. There is not one kind of logic for the world and another for the spirit, but the same logic is applicable to both. Men faithfully, and with unerring worldly wisdom, observe certain laws or rules of action in material things, knowing that to ignore or disobey them would be great folly on their part, ending in disaster for themselves and confusion for society and the state, but they err in supposing and believing that the same rules do not apply in spiritual things, and thereby suffer for their ignorance and disobedience.

It is a law in worldly things that a man shall support himself, that he shall earn his living, and that "He that will not work, neither shall he eat." Men observe this law, recognising its justice and goodness, and so earn the necessary material sustenance. But in spiritual things men, broadly speaking, deny and ignore the operation of this law. They think that, while it is absolutely just that a man should earn his material bread, and that the man who shirks this law should wander in rags and want, it is right that they should beg for their spiritual bread, think it to be just that they should receive all spiritual blessings without either deserving or attempting to earn them. The result is that most men wander in spiritual beggary and want— that is, in suffering and sorrow—deprived of spiritual sustenance, of joy and knowledge and peace. If you are in need of any worldly thing—food, clothing, furniture, or other necessary—you do not beg of the storekeeper to give it to you; you ask the price of it, pay for it with your money, and then it becomes your own. You recognise the perfect justice in giving an equivalent for what you receive, and would not wish it to be otherwise. The same just law prevails in spiritual things. If you are in need of any spiritual thing—joy, assurance, peace, or whatelse soever—you can only come into full possession of it by giving an equivalent; you must pay the price for it. As you must give a portion of your material substance for a worldly thing so you must give a portion of your immaterial substance for a spiritual thing. You must yield up some passion or lust or vanity or indulgence before the spiritual possession can be yours. The miser who clings to his money and will not give up any of it because of the pleasure which its possession affords him cannot have any of the material comforts of life. He lives in continual want and discomfort in spite of all his wealth. The man who will not give up his passions, who clings to anger, unkindness, sensuality, pride, vanity, self-indulgence, for the momentary pleasure which their gratification affords him is a spiritual miser; he cannot have any spiritual comforts, and suffers continual spiritual want and uneasiness in spite of the wealth of worldly pleasures which he fondly hugs and refuses to give up.

The man who is wise in worldly things neither begs nor steals, but labours and purchases, and the world honours him for his uprightness. The man who is wise in spiritual things neither begs nor steals, but labours in his own inner world, and purchases his spiritual possessions. Him the whole universe honours for his righteousness.

It is another law in worldly things that a man who engages himself to another in any form of employment shall be content with the wages upon which he agreed. If at the end of his week's work, and on receiving his wages, he were to ask his employer for a larger sum, pleading that, though he could not justly claim it and did not really deserve it, yet he expected it, he would not only not receive the larger sum but would, doubtless, be discharged from his post. Yet in spiritual things men do not think it to be either foolish or selfish to ask for those blessings—spiritual wages—upon which they never agreed, for which they never laboured, and which they do not deserve. Every man gets from the law of the universe that upon which he agrees and for which he works—no more, no less; and he is continually entering into agreements with the Supreme Law—the Master of the universe. For every thought and act which he gives he receives its just equivalent; for all work done in the form of deeds he receives the wages due to him. Knowing this, the enlightened man is always content, always satisfied, and in perfect peace, knowing that whatever he receives (be it that men call misfortune or good fortune) he has earned. The Great Law never cheats any man of his just due, but it says to the railer and the complainer "Friend didst thou not agree with me for a penny a day?"

Again, if a man would grow rich in worldly goods he must economise, and husband his financial resources until he has accumulated sufficient capital to invest in some branch of industry; then he must judiciously invest his little store of capital, neither holding it too tightly nor letting it go carelessly. He thus increases both in worldly wisdom and worldly riches. The idle spendthrift cannot grow rich; he is wasteful and riotous. He who would grow rich in spiritual things must also economise, and husband his mental resources. He must curb his tongue and his impulses, not wasting his energy in idle gossip, vain argument, or excesses of temper. In this way he will accumulate a little store of wisdom which is his spiritual capital, and this he must send out into the world for the good of others, and the more he uses it the richer will he become. Thus does a man increase in both heavenly wisdom and heavenly riches. The man who follows his blind impulses and desires and does not control and govern his mind is a spiritual spendthrift. He can never become rich in divine things.

It is a physical law that if we would reach the summit of a mountain we must climb thither. The path must be sought and then carefully followed, and the climber must not give up and go back because of the labour involved and the difficulties to be overcome, nor on account of aching climbs, otherwise his object cannot be accomplished. And this law is also spiritual. He who would reach the high altitudes of moral or intellectual grandeur must climb thither by his own efforts. He must seek out the pathway and then assiduosly follow it, not giving up and turning back, but surmounting all difficulties, and enduring for a time trials, temptations, and heartaches, and at last he will stand upon the glorious summit of moral perfection, the world of passion, temptation, and sorrow beneath his feet, and the boundless heavens of dignity stretching vast and silent above his head.

If a man would reach a distant city, or any place of destination, he must travel thither. There is no law by which he can be instantly transported there. He can only get there by putting forth the necessary exertion. If he walks he will put forth great exertion, but it will cost him nothing in money; if he drives or takes train, there will be less actual labour, but he must pay in money for which he has laboured. To reach any place requires labour; this cannot be avoided; it is law. Equally so spiritually. He who would reach any spiritual destination, such as purity, compassion, wisdom, or peace, must travel thither, and must labour to get there. There is no law by which he can suddenly be transported to any of these beautiful spiritual cities. He must find the most direct route and then put forth the necessary labour, and at last he will come to the end of his journey.

These are but a few of the many laws, or manifestations of the One Great Law, which are to be understood, applied and obeyed before the full manhood and maturity of spiritual life and blessedness can be attained. There is no worldly or physical law which is not operative, with equal exactness, in the spiritual realm—that is, the inner and invisible world of man's beings. Just as physical things are the shadows and types, of spiritual realities so worldly wisdom is the reflected image of Divine Wisdom. All those simple operations of human life in worldly things which men never question, but follow and obey implicitly because of their obvious plainness and exactness, obtain in spiritual things with the same unerring accuracy; and when this is understood, and these laws are as implicitly obeyed in spiritual as in worldly matters, then has a man reached the firm standing-ground of exact knowledge; his sorrows are at an end, and he can doubt no more.

Life is uninvolved, uncompromising justice; its operations are simple, invincible logic. Law reigns for ever, and the heart of law is love. Favouritism and caprice are the reverse of both law and love. The universe has no favourites; it is supremely just, and gives to every man his rightful earnings. All is good because all is according to law, and because all is according to law, man can find the right way in life, and, having found it, can rejoice and be glad. The Father of Jesus is the Unfailing Good which is embodied in the law of things. "No evil can happen to a good man either in life or death." Jesus recognised the good in his own fate, and exonerated all his persecutors from blame. "No man," he declared, "taketh my life from me, but I lay it down of myself." That is, he himself had brought about his own end.

He who has, by simplifying his life and purifying his mind, arrived at an understanding of the beautiful simplicity of being, perceives the unvarying operation of law in all things, and knows the result of all his thoughts and deeds upon himself and the world—knows what effects are bound up with the mental causes which he sets in motion. He then thinks and does only those thoughts and deeds that are blessed in their inception, blessed in their growth, and blessed in their completion. Humbly accepting the lawful results of all the deeds done when in a state of ignorance, he neither complains nor fears nor questions, but is at rest in obedience, is perfectly blessed in his knowledge of the Good Law.

"The tissue of our life to be
We weave with colours all our own,
And in the field of Destiny
We reap as we have sown.
And if we reap as we have sown,
And take the dole we deal,
The law of pain is love alone,
The wounding is to heal."

HAPPY ENDINGS

"Such is the Law which moves to righteousness,
Which none at last can turn aside or stay;
The heart of it is Love, the end of it
Is peace and consummation sweet. Obey."
—The Light of Asia.

"So, haply, when thy task shall end,
The wrong shall lose itself in right,
And all thy week-day Sabbaths blend
With the long Sabbath of the Light!"
—Whittier

Life has many happy endings, because it has much that is noble and pure and beautiful. Although there is much sin and ignorance in the world, many tears, and much pain and sorrow, there is also much purity and knowledge, many smiles, and much healing and gladness. No pure thought, no unselfish deed can fall short of its felicitous result, and every such result is a happy consummation.

A pleasant home is a happy ending; a successful life is a happy ending; a task well and faithfully done is a happy ending; to be surrounded by kind friends is a happy ending. A quarrel put away, grudges wiped out, unkind words confessed and forgiven, friend restored to friend—all these are happy endings. To find that which one has long and tediously sought; to be restored from tears to gladness; to awaken in the bright sunlight out of the painful nightmare of sin, to strike, after much searching, the Heavenly Way in life—these are, indeed, blessed consummations.

He who looks for, finds, and enters the byways which I have indicated will come to this one without seeking it, for his whole life will be filled with happy endings. He who begins right and continues right does not need to desire and search for felicitous results; they are already at hand; they follow as consequences; they are the certainties, the realities of life.

There are happy endings which belong solely to the material world; these are transient, and they pass away. These are happy endings which belong to the spiritual world; these are eternal, and they do not pass away. Sweet are companionships, pleasures, and material comforts, but they change and fade away. Sweeter still are Purity, Wisdom, and the knowledge of Truth, and these never change nor fade away. Wherever a man goes in this world he can take his worldly possessions with him; but soon he must part company with them, and if he stands upon these alone, deriving all his happiness from them, he will come to a spiritual ending of great emptiness and want. But he has attained to the possession of spiritual things can never be deprived of his source of happiness: he will never have to part company with it, and wherever he goes in the whole universe he will carry his possession with him. His spiritual end will be the fullness of joy.

Happy in the Eternal Happiness is he who has come to that Life from which the thought of self is abolished. Already, even now and in this life, he has entered the Kingdom of Heaven, Nirvana, Paradise, the New Jerusalem, the Olympus of Jupiter, the Valhalla of the Gods. He knows the Final Unity of Life, the Great Reality of which these fleeting and changing names are but feeble utterances. He is at rest on the bosom of the Infinite.

Sweet is the rest and deep the bliss of him who has freed his heart from its lusts and hatreds and dark desires; and he who, without any shadow of bitterness or selfishness resting upon him, and looking out upon the world with boundless compassion and love, can breathe, in his inmost heart, the blessing:

Peace unto all living things,

making no exceptions or distinctions—such a man has reached that happy ending which can never be taken away, for this is the perfection of life, the fullness of peace, the consummation of perfect blessedness.